KNITWEAR
FASHION
DESIGN

Copyright © 2013: Zahorí de Ideas
Copyright © 2013 for the current edition :
Promopress
Copyright © 2013 for text and illustrations:
Maite Lafuente

Promopress is a commercial brand of:
Promotora de prensa internacional S.A.
C/ Ausias March 124
08013 Barcelona (Spain)
T: (+34) 93 245 14 64
F: (+34) 93 265 48 93
mail: info@promopress.es
www.promopresseditions.com

Author & Illustrator: Maite Lafuente
Editor: Satèl·lit bcn
Layout & design: Meri Iannuzzi
Foreword: Charo Mora
Collaborators: Lanas Katia, Bernabé Martínez (technician), Esther Santamaria (knitwear workshop), Ramón Vilalta (spinner).
English translation: Linda Robins da Silva and Hugo Steckelmacher

ISBN: 978-84-92810-62-8

Printed in China

First edition in English: 2013

All rights reserved. Total or partial reproduction of this work, by any means or procedure, and the distribution of copies by way of hire or lending is strictly forbidden without the copyright holder's authorization, under the sanctions established by law.

All the images in this book have been reproduced with the knowledge and prior consent of the artists concerned. Every effort has been made to ensure that credits accurately match the information supplied. In the event of any omissions or errors, the publisher would be pleased to make the appropriate correction for future editions of the book.

MAITE LAFUENTE

KNIT-WEAR FASHION DESIGN

promopress

INDEX

0 **FOREWORD** 06
Charo Mora

1 **TOP FASHION KNITWEAR DESIGNERS** 10

2 **ESSENTIAL YARNS** 24
TYPOLOGIES / KNITTED YARNS

3 **BASIC STITCHES** 54

4 **ILLUSTRATED STITCHES AND GARMENTS** 60

5 **ACCESSORIES** 118

6 **REVAMPING THE BASICS** 134

7 **SPECIFICATION SHEETS** 152

8 **GLOSSARY** 156

FORE-
WORD

THE POETICS OF KNITWEAR

Knitwear is by nature curved, like the contours of the body, and this explains its particular ability to seamlessly adjust to and fit different body shapes, like a second skin. This property has placed this type of fabric, which is as old as mankind, at the undisputed forefront of modern clothing, even to a certain extent becoming its metaphor. The key lies in its comfort – above and beyond its other properties, knitwear wraps itself around the body, clinging to it, a quality that has seen it take on a starring role in the fashion world of the 20th and 21st centuries.

Outdoor sport playing, a habit taken up by the privileged classes in the first few decades of the 20th century, gave rise to a new "vocabulary" for fashion in which luxury and comfort went hand in hand. Almost all of the top designers of the time, including Patou, Lanvin, Vionnet and later Schiaparelli, opened up their own stores and created ranges dedicated to sport featuring a wide array of garments fashioned out of this snug fabric. Pieces designed for tennis courts or the golf course quickly broke out of these exclusive confines and landed in the street, where they were destined to remain. It is difficult to understand 20th-century fashion without considering the impact of Patou's knitwear pyjamas, designed in the 20s for use on cruise ships, or Schiaparelli's tennis sweaters. This notwithstanding, it was the world of work, rather than leisure, that definitively changed the face of 20th-century fashion. Contemporary men and women sported a wardrobe that, while functional, was no less sensual or attractive, and it was knitwear that made this possible. The twinset, the cardigan and the sweater emerged as permanent fixtures of the wardrobe, over time gaining the status of essentials. Their increasing prominence is evidenced by the fact that in the 50s the production of knitwear almost matched that of flat-woven fabrics.

Indeed, the possibilities offered by knitwear are endless. We wear it, sure enough, but it can also be used to draw or even sculpt with. Gabrielle Chanel was probably the first designer to use this type of fabric to make outerwear. Her iconic dresses and two-piece suits, back in the 20s, are a wonderful example of this contribution. In the 30s, Schiaparelli fashioned her famous skeleton sweaters and *trompe l'oeil* pieces, with their elaborate fibres, while in the 21st century the Swedish designer Sandra Backlund's fascinating garments show knitwear at its most sculptural. However, as depicted in the pages of this book, knitwear is also a form of expression. In the hands of designers, this type of fabric inspires experimentation and stimulates the imagination. It is an expanding universe which, to quote my preliminary correspondence with the author prior to writing this foreword, "has still only explored the half of its creative possibilities". This volume will allow you to gain a much deeper appreciation of knitwear and, above all, to learn how to illustrate it. After being introduced to its secrets, peculiarities and history, nimble readers will be able to translate their imaginations into design and their thoughts into reality. Herein lies the originality and beauty of this volume. More than two years in the making, its content above all owes itself to the author's over thirty years of knowledge and experience relating to the world of knitting. As such, the book offers a real insider's view of the nature of knitwear, from the technical aspects to its more creative dimension. It is an invitation to discover the essence of knitwear and shape its future.

CHARO MORA SOLANILLA

Holder of a Degree in History of Art from the University of Barcelona, since 1998 Charo Mora Solanilla has been working as a fashion journalist and a Professor of History of Fashion and Emerging Trends at the Escola Superior de Disseny (ESDi/Universitat Ramón Llull). As a curator and researcher, she has been involved in several major projects, including curating the fashion section at the *BAC Barcelona Contemporary Art Festival* in 2003 and 2004, the exhibition *Santa Eulalia: espíritu de mujer*, in 2005, and the *Carte Blanche* section of the 2012 Barcelona edition of the *A Shaded View on Fashion Film* (ASVOFF) festival, held at the CaixaForum. She is also a correspondent for Barcelona-based magazine *Yo Dona* and a fashion consultant for the international publication *Metal Magazine*.

TOP FASHION KNITWEAR DESIGNERS

The great fashion designers have left a valuable legacy in the field of knitwear, from Schiaparelli's *trompe l'oeil* in the early 20th century through Rykiel's graphic knits in the 70s and Sandra Backlund's hand-crafted sculptural pieces of the 2000s. We have witnessed an immensely innovative evolution in knitwear - in its forms, techniques, volumes, structures and materials - driven by a surge of diverse ideas that continue to set the bar today and must necessarily be revisited prior to any attempt to design collections for a new season. Besides examining each creator's contribution to the genre, the specific selection of designers set out in this tome charts the evolution of knitwear volumes, colours and textures over the years. The illustration techniques chosen for the volume - namely pencil, graphite, watercolour and felt-tip pen - together with the figurative nature of the illustrations seek to mimic the styles of illustration prevalent in the periods explored.

ELSA SCHIAPARELLI

Trompe l'oeil
Date unknown

Born in Rome, Italy, in 1890, her career as a designer took off after meeting Paul Poiret. Her vision was to dress women in loose, functional and highly original garments that could be mixed and matched. She began to win the attention of the artists of her time as a result of her originality and, in particular, her use of surrealist principles. These include creations such as the shoe hat and gloves with golden finger nails attached to them and, where knitwear is concerned, intarsia sweaters with fake bow knits, as well as stripes in two colours, on the front: a whole world of *trompe l'oeil* images.

JEAN PATOU

Cardigan
1926-27

Born in Normandy, France, in 1880. His creations popularised loose-fitting shapes, lengthened skirts and ties for women. Sports clothes, both men's and women's, occupied a prominent place in his collections, introducing a new dimension to the world of fashion. His knit work is most famous for his creation of knitted swimwear and for spreading the use of cardigans, in conjunction with tennis-style pleated skirts. Patou's vision for his clothing involved a harmonious interplay of naturalness and comfort.

PRINGLE

Twinset
1950

Robert Pringle founded the company *Pringle of Scotland* in 1815. From the outset the Pringle brand has focused on spinning cashmere and wool threads, as well as producing knitwear. During the 1950s and 60s, it popularised the twinset, a two-piece set intended for working women, particularly secretaries and teachers. However, it was a number of Hollywood actresses, including Grace Kelly, Marilyn Monroe and especially Joan Fontaine, who sported its designs in Alfred Hitchcock's *Rebecca*, who helped cement its reputation as an international fashion icon.

COURRÈGES

Ribbed Knitwear
1960s

André Courrèges was born in Pau, France in 1923. He was recognised for the marked geometrical lines of his designs, which married simplicity and comfort with a distinctively futuristic edge. He introduced materials such as plastics, both opaque and see-through, which were highly innovative for the period, into his clothing. He also incorporated knitwear into his collections, including ribs and compact Milano stitch, which revolutionised the signature look of the time. Equally ahead of its time was the colour palette used in his creations, which ranged from white, which he turned into a fashion icon, to bold pastel shades and two-tone combinations such as red and black and black and white.

MISSONI

Zigzag
1970s

Ottavio Missoni was born in 1921 in Dubrovnik (then Ragusa), in the former Kingdom of Yugoslavia. Together with his wife Rosita Jelmini, he founded the Missoni couture house, specialising in knitwear, in 1953. In 1966 the Missoni couple presented their first collection in Milan, their fresh, modern garments revolutionising traditional knitwear and elevating their status to artistic creation. They breathed new life into the Rachel machine, which had previously been used to make shawls, in order to create their prêt-à-porter line. The originality of their zigzag designs, the blend of different knits employed and their signature colour combinations, which are impossible to imitate, are trademarks of the Missoni brand, which continues to set trends even today.

SONIA RYKIEL

Messages
Winter 1984

Having been born in Paris, France, in 1930, Sonia Rykiel started her career in fashion by designing her own maternity dresses, opening up her first boutique in 1968. She specialises in knitwear, which she has used to fashion light and simple pieces in soft wools such as angora and mohair. Her garments stand out for their sensuality and she has a preference for long, clingy sweaters and small, tight pullovers. She has also experimented with seams and hem finishes in her creations, including putting seams and printing words on the outside of her pieces. In the 1980s she popularised striped and ruffled sweaters featuring intarsia messages. Her creations have become a key benchmark for how to design a knitwear collection.

COMME DES GARÇONS

Destroyed
1982

This house was founded in 1969 by Rei Kawakubo, the Japanese designer born in Tokyo in 1942. Its designs won major plaudits in the Japanese capital in the 1970s. It enjoyed a hugely successful debut show in Paris in 1981, where its pieces created significant buzz – owing to their destroyed, austere and nihilistic look, dominated by the use of black – becoming a flag-bearer for the so-called "Japanese Revolution". The Comme des Garçons brand pioneered the creation of deconstructed knitwear, often featuring destroyed embroidery, which verges on anti-fashion. Baggy and loose-fitting, the garments can be worn alone or matched with other pieces.

AZZEDINE ALAÏA

Sexy

Born in Siliana, Tunisia, in 1940, he moved to Paris in 1957, working as a tailor for Christian Dior, before subsequently collaborating with Guy Laroche and Thierry Mugler. After eventually opening his own atelier in the late 1970s, he won a fashion Oscar for his first collection, dominated by tight, sexy garments, in 1980. His knitwear creations tend to combine synthetic threads and compact styles, such as Ponte and Milano knits, to ensure a snug fit. They also incorporate off-cuts and seams on the outside, innovatively using the coverstitch machine to adorn and mould the figure. His designs continue to be a source of inspiration for fashion lovers today.

YOHJI YAMAMOTO

Asymmetric
1992-93

Born in Tokyo, Japan, in 1943, he is renowned for his staunchly avant-garde designs, which often eschew current trends in pursuit of creativity. His signature style is characterised by oversized, seemingly unfinished garments in black, often featuring built-up layers of different fabrics and textures. The oft-imitated black and navy combination, which is vastly popular today, was his creation. He gained international recognition in the fashion world thanks to his distressed knitwear volumes, designed in 1990, and his experiments with different forms and weaves.

MAISON MARTIN MARGIELA

Highly personal
2009-10

Martin Margiela was born in Belgium in 1957. He worked with Jean Paul Gaultier from 1985 to 1987, and later served as the creative director of Hermès between 1997 and 2003, in spite of his reputation as an experimental designer. During the 1980s Margiela swam against the tide of the luxury fashion world, designing oversized creations with long arms and rethinking basic principles and elements of haute couture, including placing seams and hems on the outside of garments. His artistic production cannot be fully comprehended without reference to the concept of deconstruction, espoused by the Japanese designer Rei Kawakubo, whose philosophy Margiela's knitwear pieces emulate.

SANDRA BACKLUND

New concept
October 2008

Born in Sweden, her extraordinary artistic production revolves around the use of knitwear. Her great achievement has been to make artworks out of her garments. Her designs provide a fine example of the seamless combination of traditional craftwork techniques with the latest aesthetic trends in vogue. Backlund's hand-knitted creations employ extra-chunky wools to fashion highly sculptural pieces. The passion driving her work as an artist is to remain at once innovative, creative and provocative.

RODARTE

Openwork
2008

Sisters Kate and Mulleavy founded this brand in the Californian city of Pasadena, USA, in 2005. Rodarte's designs stand out for their meticulous detail, their original fusion of delicate and vintage elements, such as tulle, gauze and hand-dyed silks, their hand-knitted seams and their melding of different yarns. Their interwoven designs put a fresh and highly attractive spin on knitwear, thanks to the use of various types of thread, in particular mohair, wool and silk, which are open stitched so as to offer a creative reinterpretation of openwork technique. Equally innovative are their soft, harmonious colour combinations.

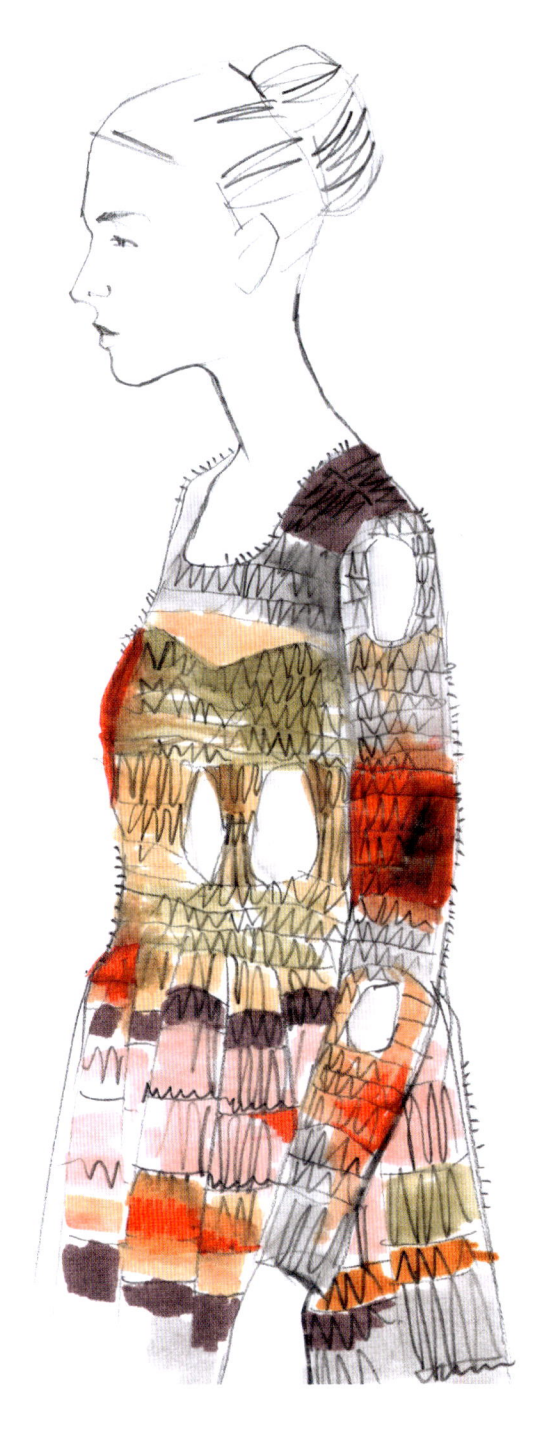

ESSEN-
TIAL
YARNS

2

Without yarn you cannot knit! Yarn is the starting point for creating a garment. You can even design your own yarn! The yarn dictates the intended thickness of the garment, the particular characteristics of the stitch, sometimes giving rise to a new size and colour, including potentially amazing tones (in the case of printed, blended or twisted yarns). If, when creating the stitch, you thoroughly examine the possibilities of each yarn, you will obtain eye-catching results and designs, and enable the yarn to stand out in a novel way in the knitted piece. In addition, changing the yarn of a garment from the previous season gives astonishing results. Indeed, by simply modifying this detail, a different and free look can be achieved. Although there is an extremely wide range of yarns, this chapter sets out only a very specific selection of the most representative of those currently available. This sample ranges from bouclé to more modest fancy yarns, such as twisted and crêpe yarns, amongst others, before moving on to slub yarns, looped yarns and tweeds, finishing off with the latest new yarns on the market. The aim is threefold: to show the structure of the yarn as it is, un-knitted; to show a real image of the knitted yarn in plain stitch and lastly, to very briefly illustrate the most suitable technique for each yarn.

Round yarn four ends

Two-colour twisted yarn

Twisted yarn with lurex

Crêpe

Slub

Thick blended wicking yarn

Loop yarn

Napped loop yarn

Mohair

Crimped yarn

Knotted yarn

Multicolour tweed

ESSENTIAL YARNS · TYPOLOGIES **KNITWEAR FASHION DESIGN**

Tape yarn

Metallic tape yarn

Binary

Chenille

Covered yarn

Lurex

28 KNITWEAR FASHION DESIGN ESSENTIAL YARNS · TYPOLOGIES

Vigoureux circular yarn

Twisted slub wicking yarn

Raschel covered yarn

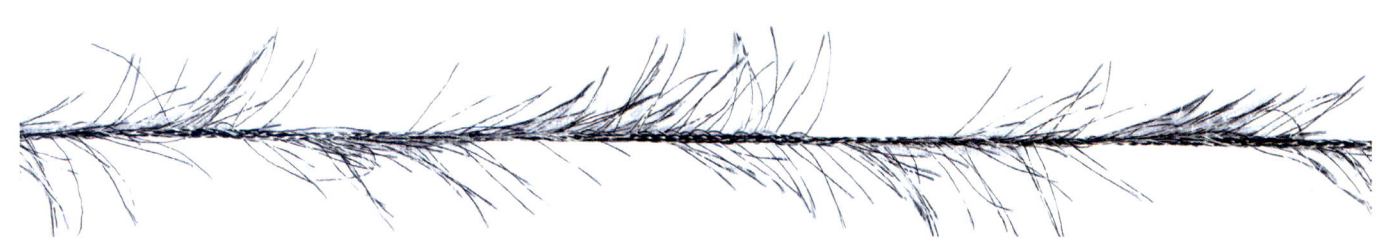

Plush yarn

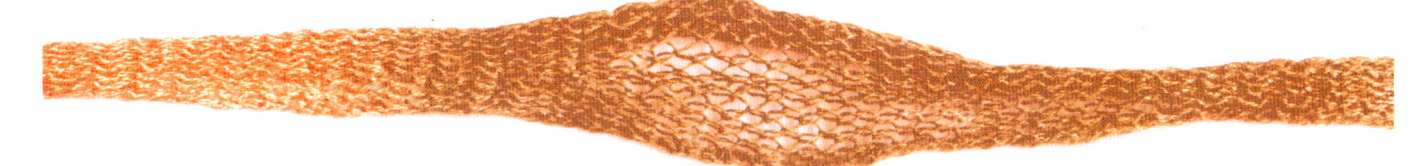

Printed mesh yarn

Raschel pom-pom yarn

ESSENTIAL YARNS · TYPOLOGIES **KNITWEAR FASHION DESIGN**

LOOP YARN

Fancy yarn made of various components, including the foundation fibre, of which an excess is fed through to form loops when twisted.

The yarn is made in various thicknesses, although 3 gg and 5 gg are the most commonly used, as they allow for the completion of the few stitches that can be done in fancy yarn: any thicker and the accumulation of loops obscures the view of the stitch. It can be used plain as well as blended with almost any design and is mainly intended for the female market and children's wear. This yarn is suitable for pieces which are simple yet bulky.

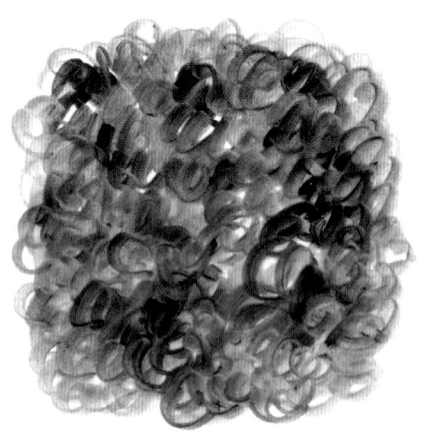

Loose-fitting garment with a wide roll-neck, and dropped shoulders.

NAPPED LOOP YARN

Fancy yarn made of various components, which is put though a napping machine once in order to break the loops and shred the foundation fibre.

When knitted in plain stitch, which is not too tight, in 3 gg or 5 gg, a bulky yet lightweight garment is obtained, similar to mohair, but without the hair, and with a similar appearance to felt. This is ideal for openwork stitches although these must be knitted in large or, even better, geometrical designs, so they can be better seen in the finished piece.

Deceptively simple dress made with an innovative pattern. The big sleeves offer a contrast to the rest of the garment.

CHENILLE

Fancy yarn made of two tightly twisted fibres that are the foundation for small sheared pieces of a third fibre.

When it is knitted up it has the appearance of velvet and is usually somewhat lustrous. All gauges are suitable for this yarn which can be made of silk, viscose or cotton. As this is a yarn covered in short hairs, micro stitches cannot be knitted. It is usually worked in openwork or large drop stitches, although it also suits being knitted in plain stitch or in fine rib stitch. This yarn is suitable for women's wear, particularly party wear.

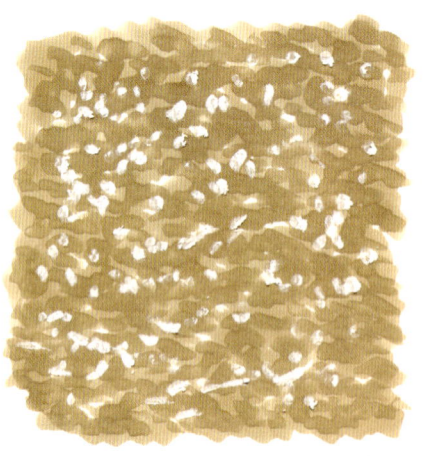

34 **KNITWEAR FASHION DESIGN** ESSENTIAL YARNS · KNITTED YARNS

Loose-fitting knee-length dress, dropped armholes, low round neck and a novel detail: longer at the back. Wide ribbing at the hems and cuffs.

ESSENTIAL YARNS · KNITTED YARNS **KNITWEAR FASHION DESIGN**

SLUB

Fancy yarn obtained by intermittently varying the drafting of one bundle of fibres onto the next. The yarns are suitable for all gauges and compositions.

They work very well when knitted in 3 gg or 5 gg and with rough matt wool, as the unevenness of the yarn is shown off and usually gives a fresh looking finish, very characteristic of this style of knitting. They are often worked with fine gauges, especially with light yarns. When knitted they have a subtle wave that, when used with material with a sheen, looks like shop-bought lingerie. They can be knitted in all stitches: however, to show off the slub of the yarn, the best stitch is a tight stocking stitch.

Very simple loose-fitting sweater with draped roll-neck, in the same fabric as the garment.

ESSENTIAL YARNS · KNITTED YARNS **KNITWEAR FASHION DESIGN**

TWEED

Carded yarn made up by the incorporation of leftover fibres of various colours.

Due to its sober appearance, this yarn has mainly been used in men's wear, however over the years and with changes in fashion, it has been adapted to the women's and children's markets. When it is hand knitted in 3 gg or 5 gg, very good results are obtained, especially for winter clothes. It is a yarn which is suitable for all types of stitches, but really stands out in raised patterns such as pearl, cable, diamonds etc.

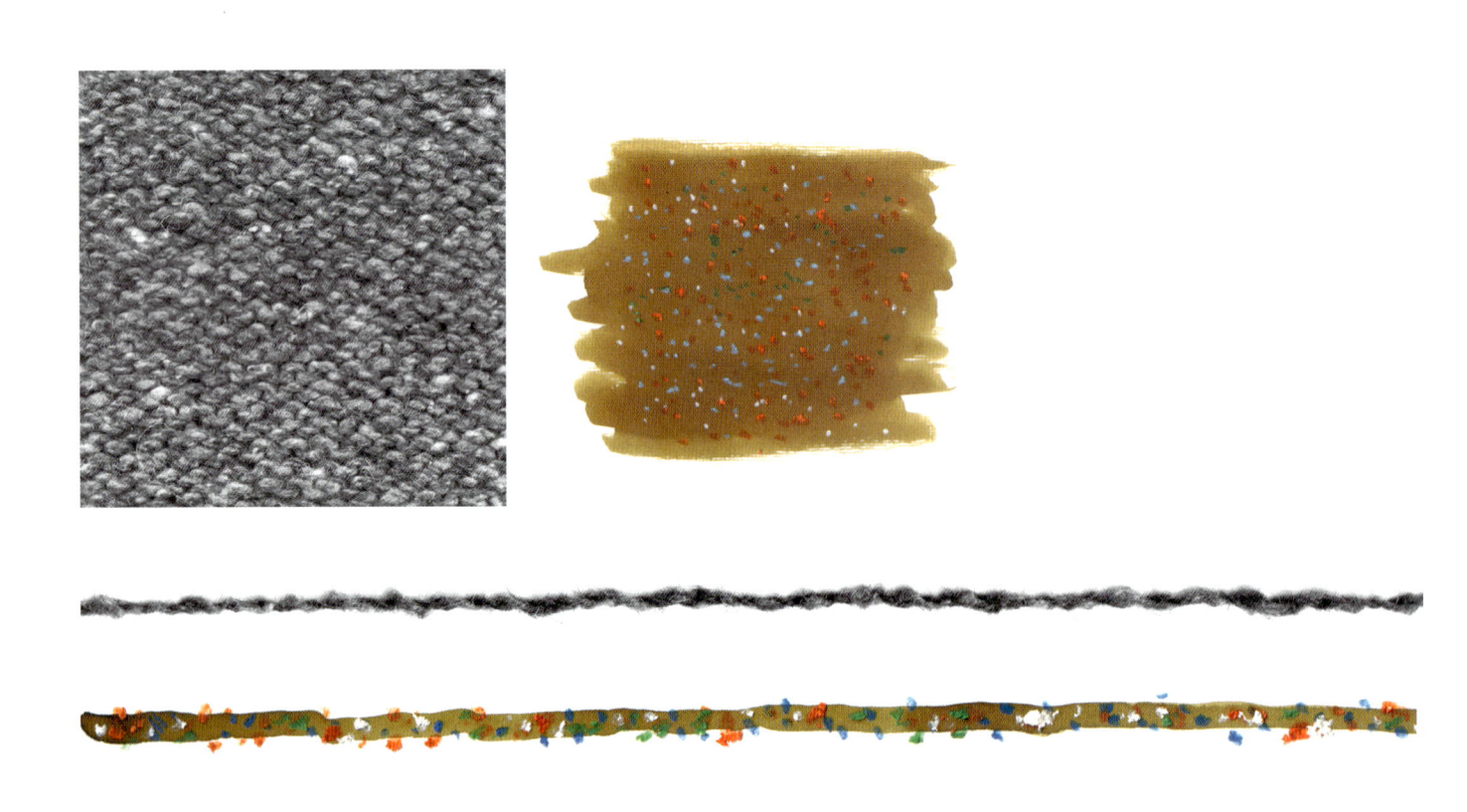

Extra wide sweater with raglan sleeves, in a thick gauge, with a distinctive cable on the front. Open roll-neck, in the same knit as the garment.

ESSENTIAL YARNS - KNITTED YARNS **KNITWEAR FASHION DESIGN**

MOHAIR

Fancy yarn made of various components with mohair as the foundation fibre so that when it is napped a long smooth hair is obtained.

It is suitable for lightweight bulky garments. Coats, jackets, sweaters and even dresses made in this yarn, whether smooth or blended, look very eye-catching. It is also often used for parts such as cuffs, flaps and, necks. For this yarn, all gauges are suitable, as are plain, slightly raised and open stitches.

40 **KNITWEAR FASHION DESIGN** ESSENTIAL YARNS - KNITTED YARNS

A boat neck, fitted shape and three-quarter length sleeves are all that are needed to show off mohair.

TWISTED YARN WITH LUREX

Yarn that is the result of twisting two or more fibres together, with one of these being lurex film.

One of the best ways to give a touch or dash of shine to knitted clothes is by using twisted thread. If the shiny lurex is covered with a mohair fibre then a delicate lustre will be obtained. This yarn can be worked in heavy and fine gauges and is intended for making party and street wear.

Maxi dress with large roll-neck and elasticated cuffs.

LUREX

Thin metallic polyester film, in this case used to make a tubular tape.

Lurex is a fine and very shiny yarn. It is usually used for party wear, although recent fashion trends have seen it used in street wear. This yarn is intended to be used to make women's clothes, both complete garments and parts, such as highlights, cuffs, flaps, stripes and necks, so as to offer a touch of shine.

44 KNITWEAR FASHION DESIGN   ESSENTIAL YARNS · KNITTED YARNS

Classic knee-length fitted buttonless cardigan, tied with a belt made of the same knitted material.

ESSENTIAL YARNS - KNITTED YARNS **KNITWEAR FASHION DESIGN**

PLUSH YARN

Yarn made of a knitted link which supports a cut weft fibre, usually made in a small tube.

Due to its structure it can only be knitted in plain stitch in 3 gg or 5 gg. There are some finer plush yarns but the results they give are not as spectacular or interesting as those in a heavy gauge. This yarn can be coloured, smooth, matt or shiny. It can be used to knit a whole garment or just parts such as neck, cuffs, hems and sleeves.

Loose-fitting tunic sweater with low V-neck and wide sleeves.

ESSENTIAL YARNS · KNITTED YARNS **KNITWEAR FASHION DESIGN** 47

TUBULAR YARN

Fancy yarn made by knitting a (usually fine) fibre on a very small tubular knitting machine. The tape is a yarn that is usually used for summer clothes.

It is worked in 3 gg or 5 gg. Drop and geometric openwork are the stitches that work best with this yarn. It can be made of different materials including cotton and viscose. It is suitable for making roomy and loose-fitting garments.

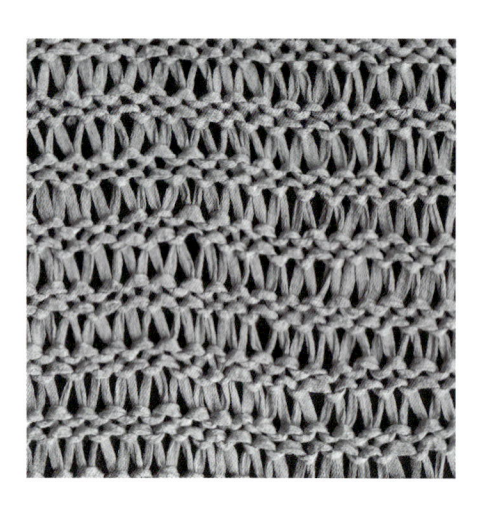

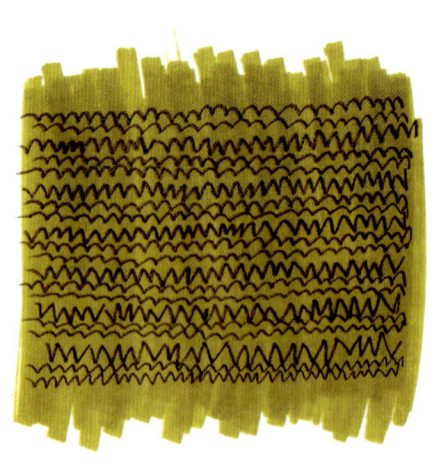

Summer garment. Loose-fitting tunic with very low boat neck and wide straight sleeves. To be worn over other garments.

RASCHEL

Thick yarn covered with two lines of chain stitch and a warp made with a Raschel machine. This is a special yarn that can be used for hand knitting and in thick gauges.

It is suitable for making garments with a hand-made appearance and accessories such as bags and scarves. Its colours can vary and it can be experimented with by combining the various colours of the inside and outside. It is usually worked in plain stitch or something similar, to obtain the best effect.

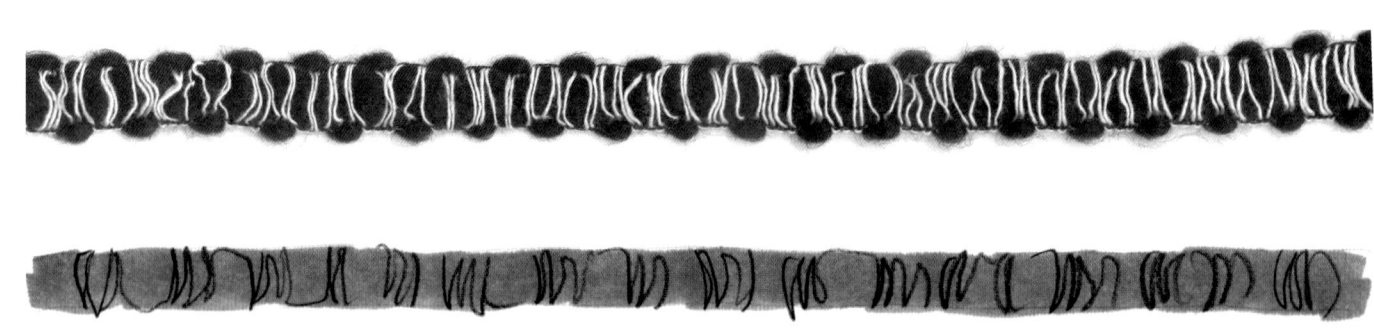

Scarf made with plaited yarn and a large bag with front flap.

ESSENTIAL YARNS · KNITTED YARNS **KNITWEAR FASHION DESIGN**

TWO-COLOUR TWISTED YARN

A yarn made from twisting two different coloured strands.

Twisted yarn can also include a combination of two or more compositions, whether similar – such as two cotton strands – or contrasting, for instance cotton and viscose, thereby achieving a simultaneously matt and shiny appearance. Likewise, the harmonies of colour can also produce different tones of a colour to create shadows, shades or contrasts. This yarn is made for all gauges and used for all seasons: however it is most often used in the winter.

Mini dress with leather belt.
Deep raglan sleeves and very low round neck.

BASIC STITCHES

3

Knitting is made up of a great number of weaves (and stitches), and still more that have yet to be discovered. In fact, one of the most attractive features of knitting is the wide creative scope which comes from different stitches. A decoration, a composition, a pattern or just about any idea which comes to mind can be turned into the basis for a sweater. Within this structural world of complex surfaces, there is a set of familiar and simpler details, well-known to designers, certain basic stitches, which must be used in a series of garments every season and need to be recognised by the people who will be the buyers of these textile products. The use of these basic stitches in new shapes and essential pieces of clothing, revamped through the colour or material, makes them look fresh and attractive. There are also examples of how to draw the stitches in a concise manner, as well as illustrations employing a more technical language.

PLAIN KNIT STITCH

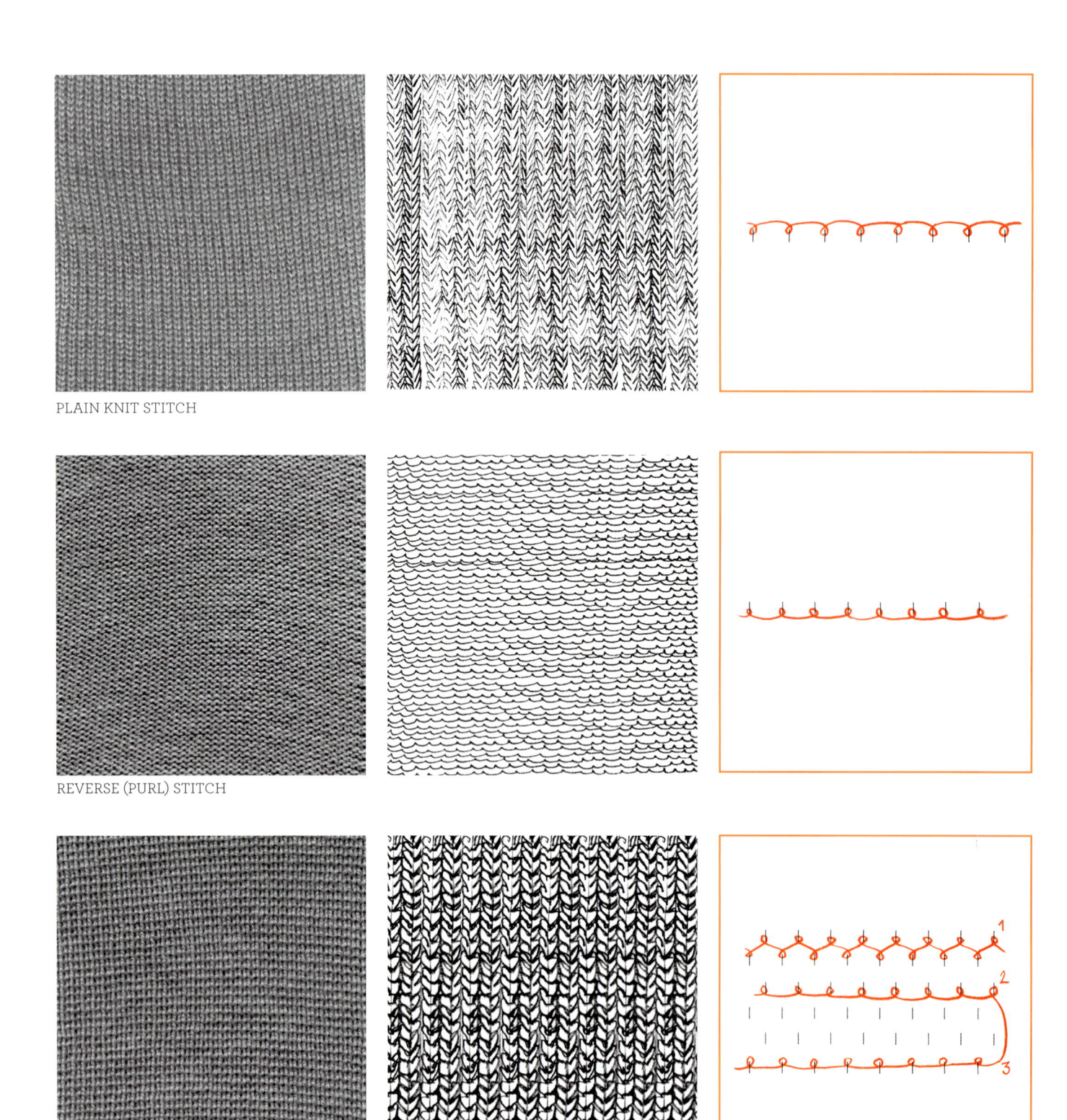

REVERSE (PURL) STITCH

ROMA STITCH

56 **KNITWEAR FASHION DESIGN** BASIC STITCHES

RIB 1X1

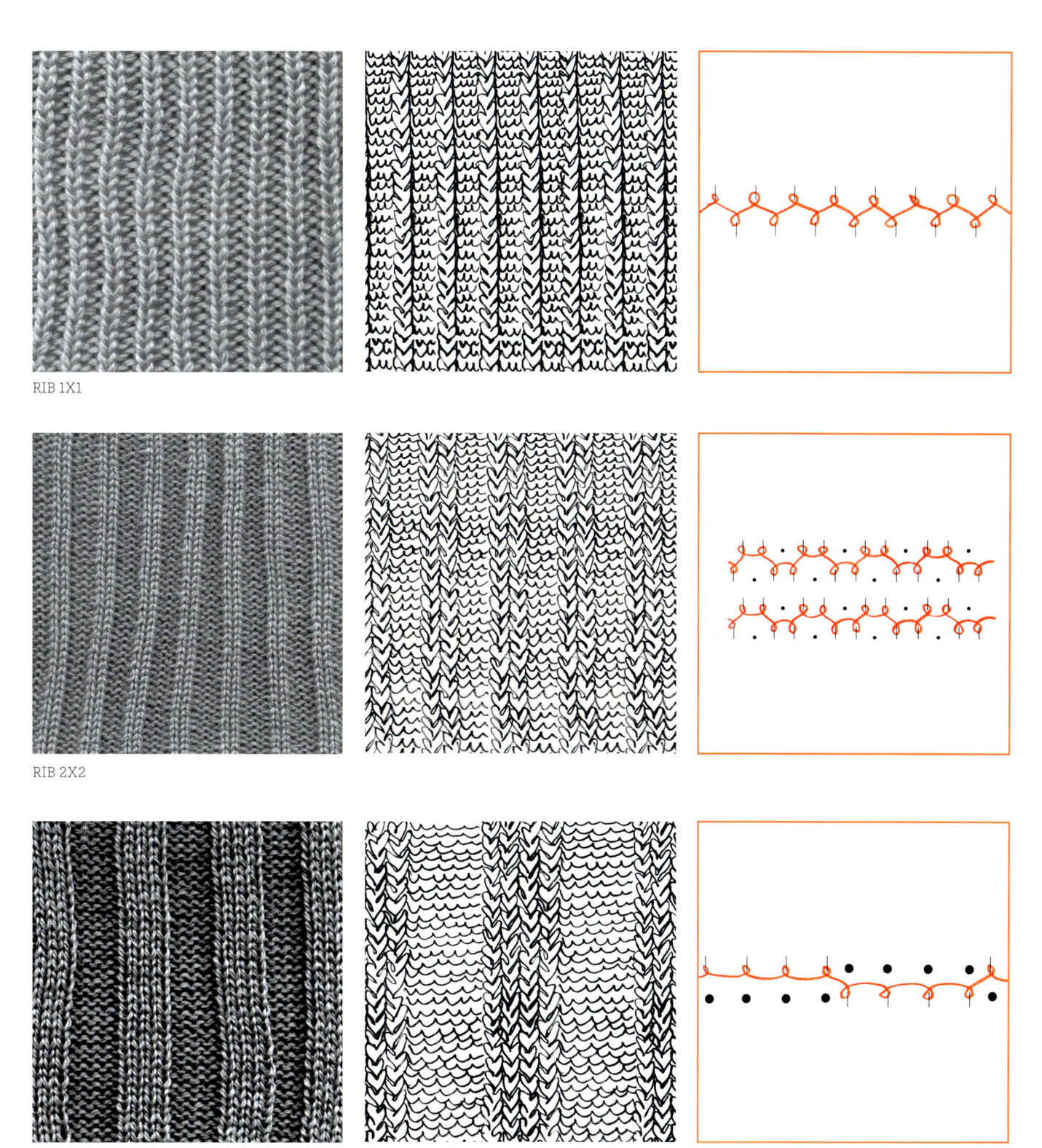

RIB 2X2

RIB 4X4

BASIC STITCHES **KNITWEAR FASHION DESIGN**

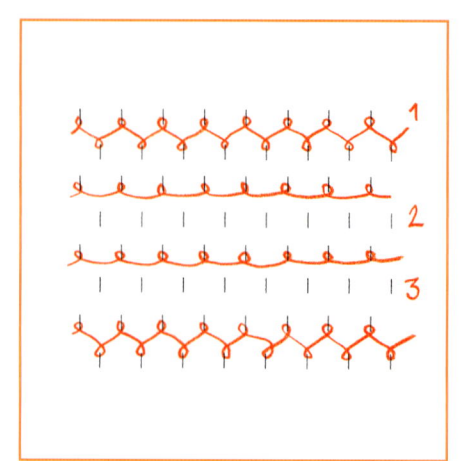

BOURRELET STITCH

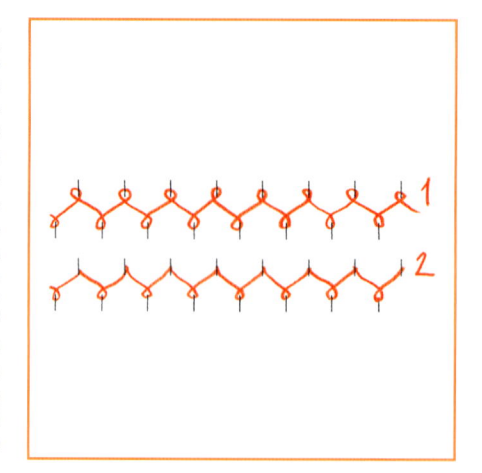

MOSS STITCH

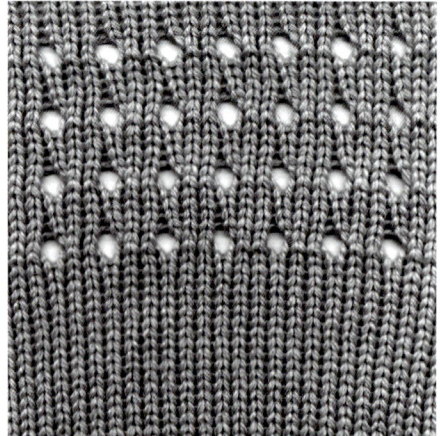

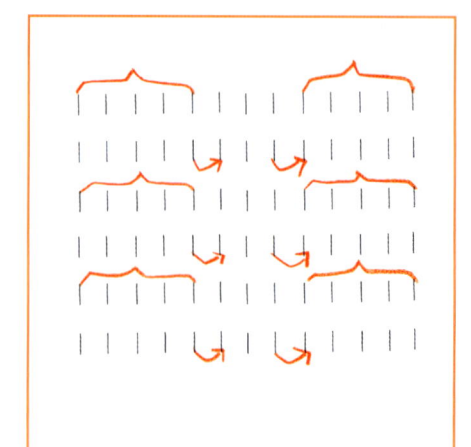

OPENWORK

58 **KNITWEAR FASHION DESIGN** BASIC STITCHES

LOOSE KNIT

LINKS

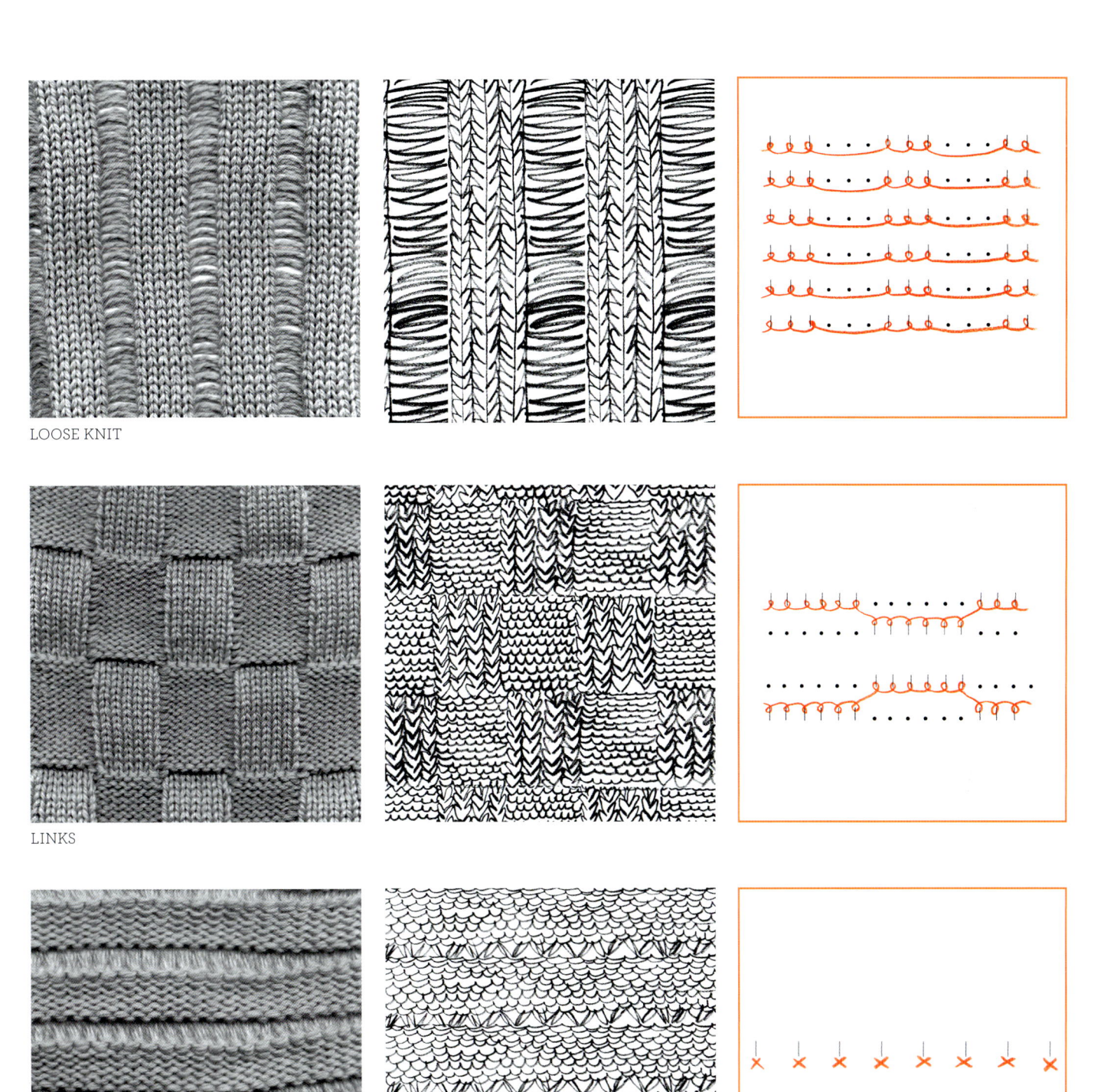

LATTICE STITCH

BASIC STITCHES **KNITWEAR FASHION DESIGN** 59

ILLUSTRATED STITCHES AND GARMENTS

The originality of the stitches is one of the reasons why some knitted garments stand out more than others. Fashion trends, the designer's individual ideas and the demands of the market are crucial at the beginning of the creative process, and together with the shape, yarn and colour they define the success of the future collection. Large patterns on small clothes, small patterns on large clothes, minimalist sweaters with basic stitches, new and hard to define over-size shapes, these and other very different ideas shown in this chapter are some of the approaches employed for textures and shapes, helped by the diversity of figurative poses illustrated in various techniques depending on the type of garment. All of this information gives a very clear and wide-ranging view of what is currently happening in the world of knitting. Likewise the flat drawings of all the clothes with their measurements give a better understanding of the product.

WRINKLED KNIT

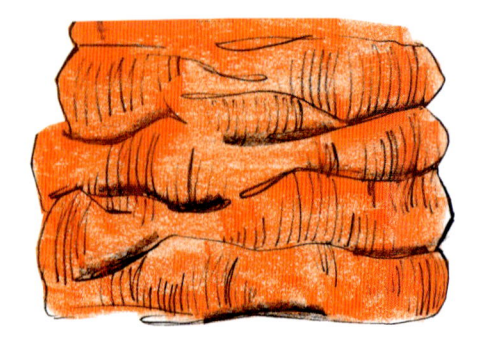

Loose-fitting three-quarter length cardigan, with dropped shoulders, tight-fitting cuffs and large shawl collar.

20

17

70

20

62 **KNITWEAR FASHION DESIGN** ILLUSTRATED STITCHES AND GARMENTS

The gathering of the knitted fabric, which is done behind the stitch, allows for the creation of a highly contemporary stitch structure, and, depending on the yarn and colour used, for the development of some very interesting shapes. The variation inside the stitch, modifying the design of the gathering of the fabric, makes it possible to achieve more original types of stitch with different looks. The original feature of this design is the stitch. It is knitted in plain round yarn and in 5 gg.

CIRCULAR

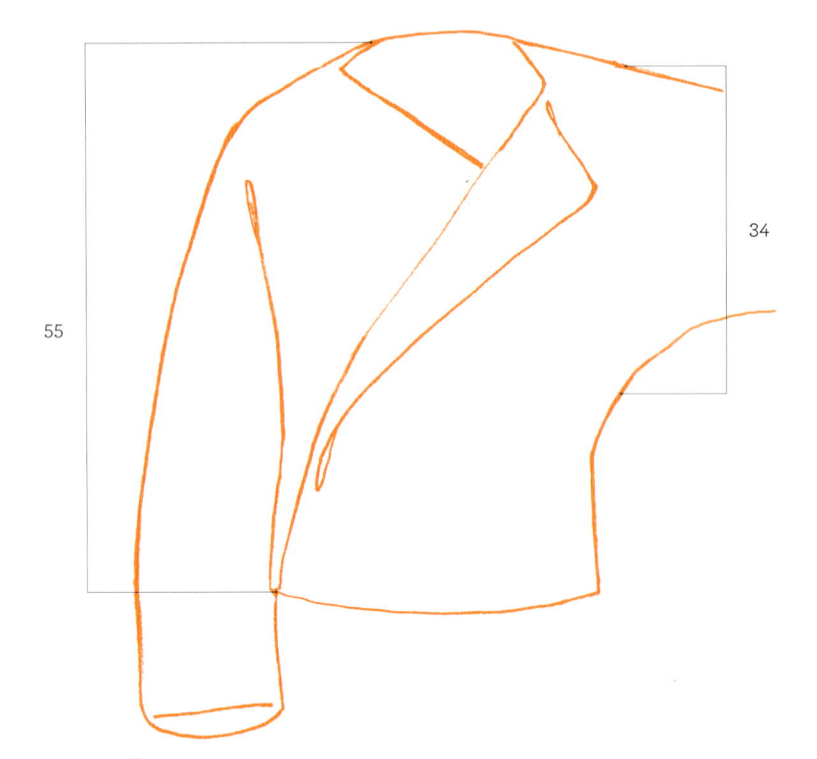

Short garment, belted at the waist, which is given a lot of volume by the yarn used. The sleeves are kimono-style and the front is crossed over to the side. The result is very simple, yet striking due to the shape and the structure of the yarn.

55

34

64 **KNITWEAR FASHION DESIGN** ILLUSTRATED STITCHES AND GARMENTS

This yarn has been made using strips of circular vigoreaux fabric, and therefore can only be knitted by hand. As its feel is dry and slightly tight, the garment drawn here has a rigid structure, devoid of detail, and the knit crosses at the front in a wrap-over style. The yarn is also suitable for knitting accessories such as bags, caps and scarves.

WAFFLE

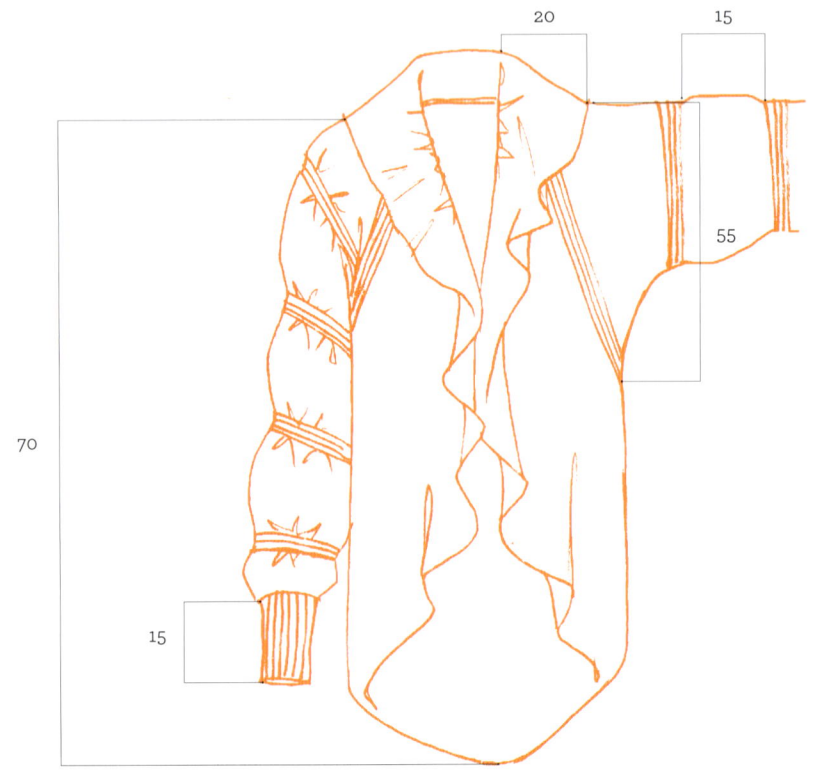

Loose-fitting three-quarter length cardigan, with dropped shoulders, fitted cuffs and large shawl collar.

66 KNITWEAR FASHION DESIGN ILLUSTRATED STITCHES AND GARMENTS

Stitch with exaggerated waffles in 5 gg. The waffle shape is used to better show off the sleeves, whilst the rest of the garment is in plain stitch. It has a large, ruffled and draped neck which continues down the front with an uneven finish. It is shorter at the front and has raglan sleeves. The garment is knitted in round woollen yarn with a touch of mohair.

3D STITCH

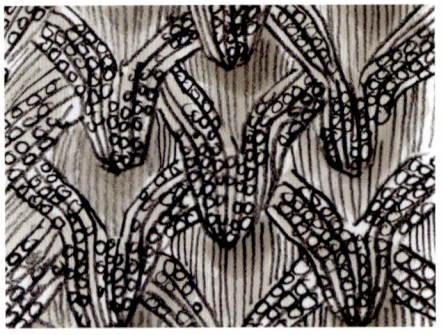

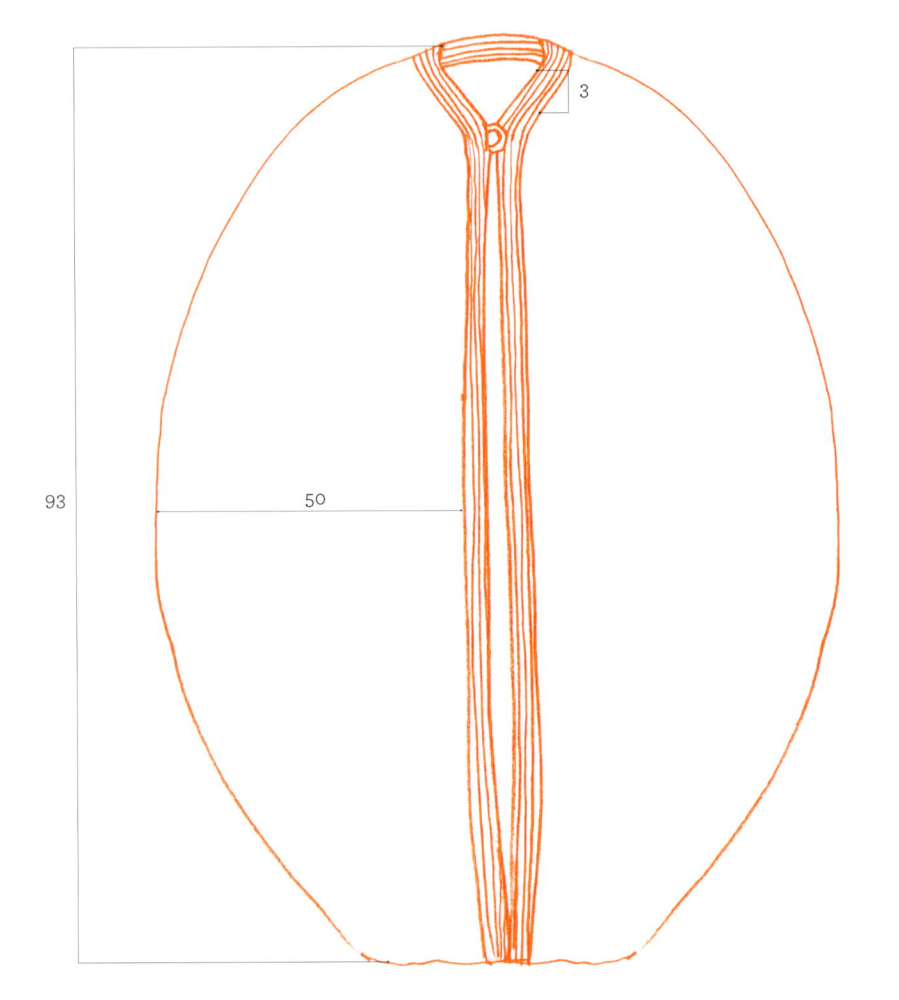

Cape with an original round, circular shape.

93

50

3

Generally, 3D stitches are used to design geometric or abstract patterns where a striking interplay of light and shadows is sought, due to the use of new yarns and novel colour combinations. 3D stitches are usually used with original shapes which differ from conventional patterns.

BOURRELET KNIT

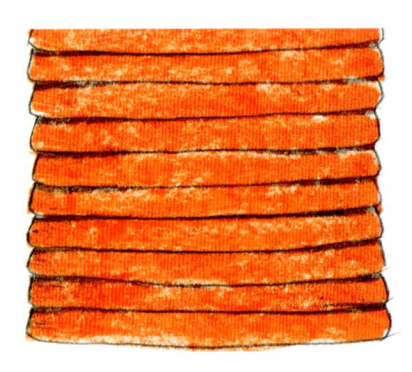

Garment in a loose-fitting design, made with bands of bourrelet stitches which have been added lengthways.

70 **KNITWEAR FASHION DESIGN** ILLUSTRATED STITCHES AND GARMENTS

Bourrelet stitches form a collection of staggered layers that can be varied in size, knitted quite tightly and, in some cases, the design can be personalised, usually in a geometrical shape. The final result is a close layered knit, a 3D stitch, which will vary depending on whether the yarn used is matt or shiny, flat or fluffy, or whether it is fancy or plain yarn.

ILLUSTRATED STITCHES AND GARMENTS **KNITWEAR FASHION DESIGN**

LOOPS

Revamped bomber jacket design: wider, longer than usual and knitted. The mandarin collar, cuffs and waistband are knitted in vertical ribs.

4

23

70

6

10

72 KNITWEAR FASHION DESIGN ILLUSTRATED STITCHES AND GARMENTS

Small loops in 3 gg are stitches which give garments a good deal of volume and a contemporary look. They are suitable for using with non-fancy yarns, ideally round, plain or blended ones. The composition can vary, but will always look better in a material with a woollen appearance.

FLOATING THREADS

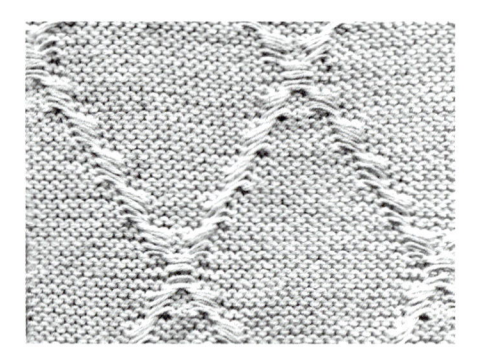

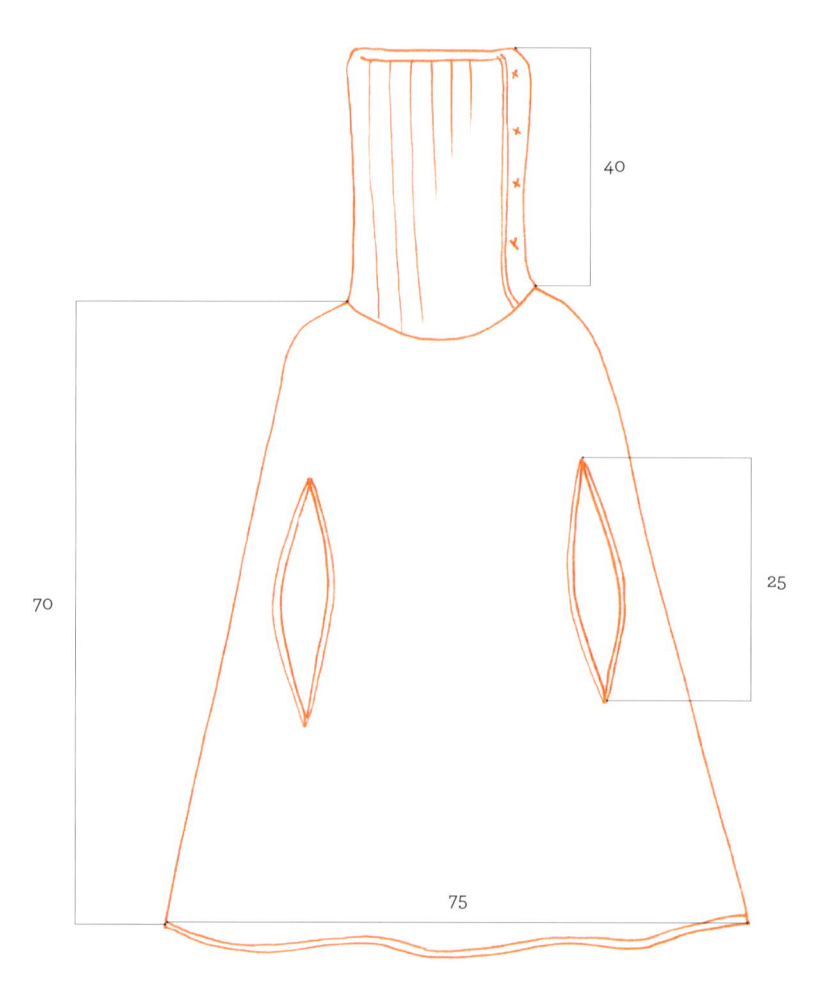

Short, loose-fitting tapered cape, with large roll-neck collar open on one side.

40

25

70

75

74 KNITWEAR FASHION DESIGN ILLUSTRATED STITCHES AND GARMENTS

These are very much in vogue, both in clean and neat designs as well as those that are casual and unstructured. In this illustration, the floating yarns trace the diamond pattern and the rest is in reverse stitch. It is knitted in round yarn, plain stitch and 5 gg.

HAZELNUT

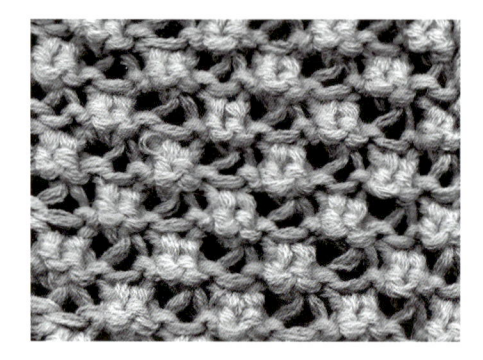

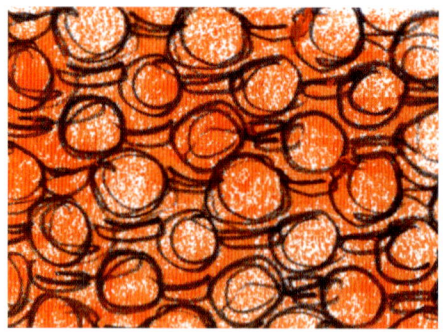

Very loose-fitting long cardigan, with belt and collar in long-haired fur. The trims, cuffs and hem are in wide 4x4 rib.

76 **KNITWEAR FASHION DESIGN** ILLUSTRATED STITCHES AND GARMENTS

This is a hand knitting stitch somewhat suggestive of raised chickpeas. Due to its rustic look, it is very popular for garments with a "hand-made" appearance such as capes, ponchos, cardigans and, of course, sweaters. This type of stitch can be done in any yarn, although it is always better to use plain yarn without any fancy elements, in order to be able to better discern the design of the knit. The composition of the yarn is not important; it can be cotton or wool. The design of the 3 gg cardigan shown here is very loose-fitting with a fur collar.

ILLUSTRATED STITCHES AND GARMENTS **KNITWEAR FASHION DESIGN**

HAZELNUT AND FLOATING YARNS

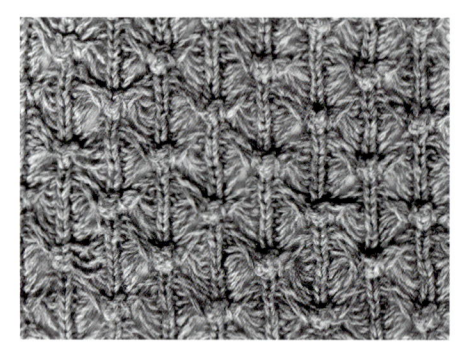

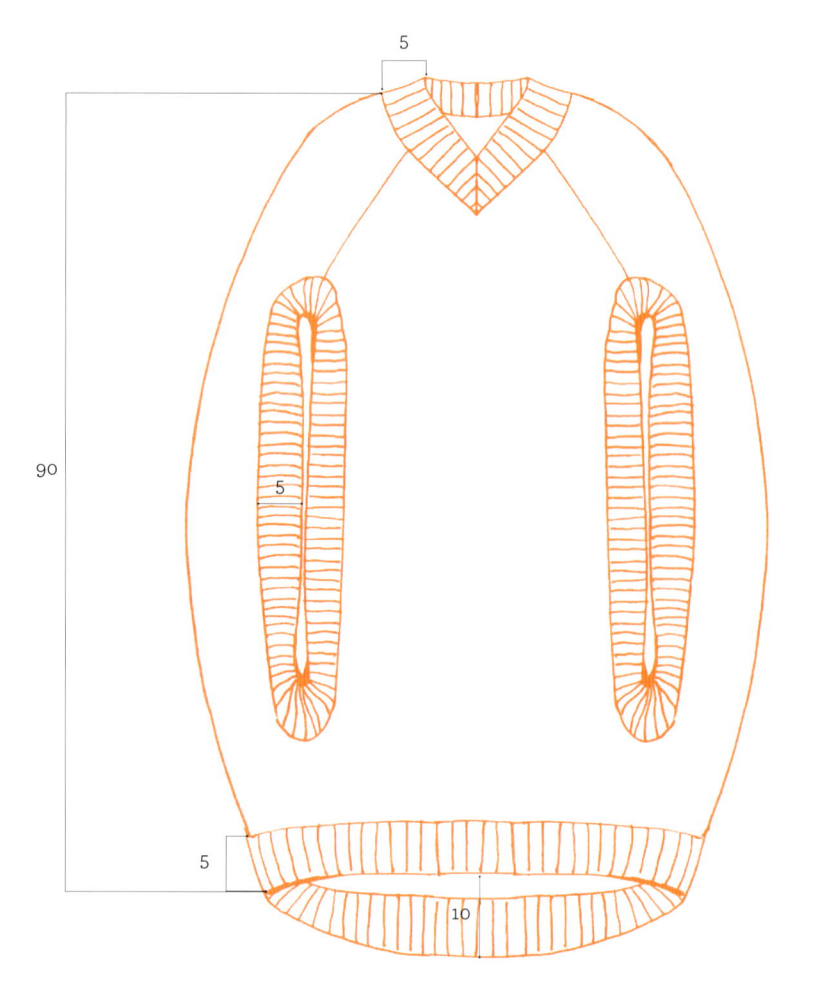

Very loose-fitting garment, in a circular shape, slightly tapered at the hem. It has large armhole openings and raglan sleeves.

78 KNITWEAR FASHION DESIGN   ILLUSTRATED STITCHES AND GARMENTS

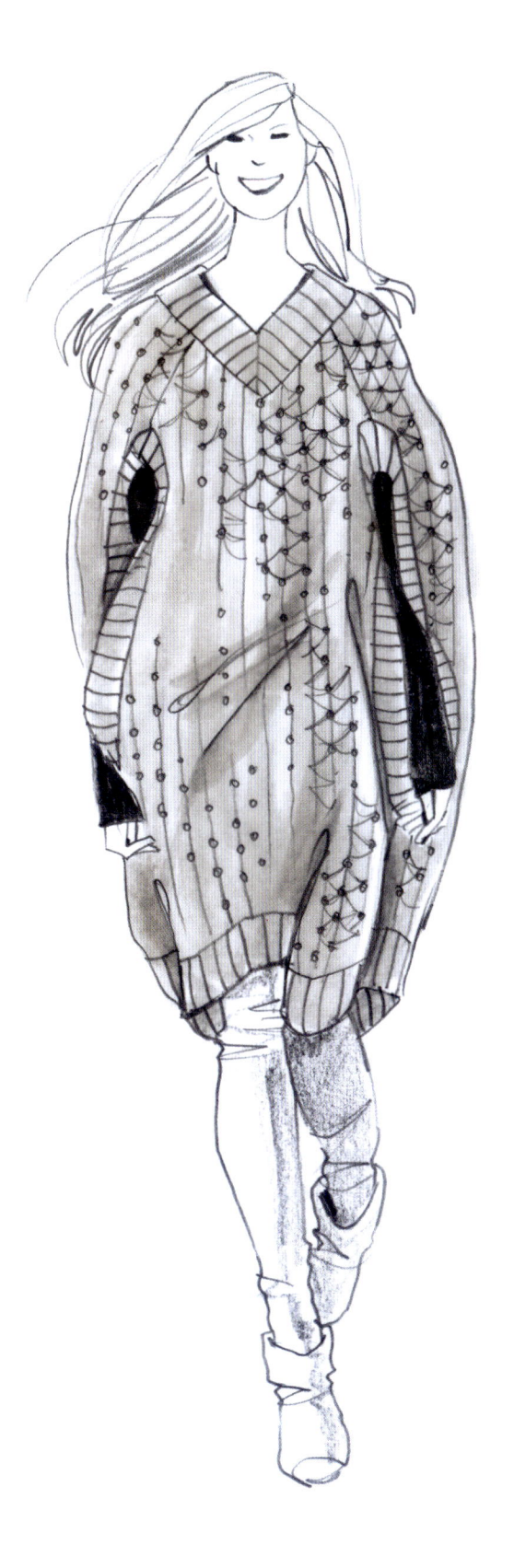

Stitch in 5 gg which combines small raised hazelnut stitches and floating yarns. It has a hand-made look and can be knitted in any type of yarn, although those with a rustic look are the most suitable. The garment is a very contemporary design that plays with the ambiguity of the dress/poncho, a new type of product that is very popular with young people.

CROSSED CABLES

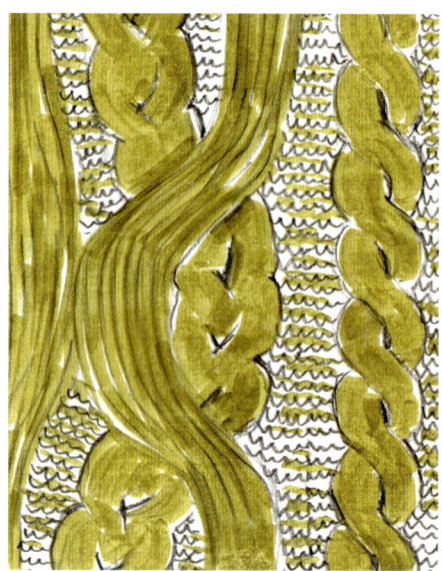

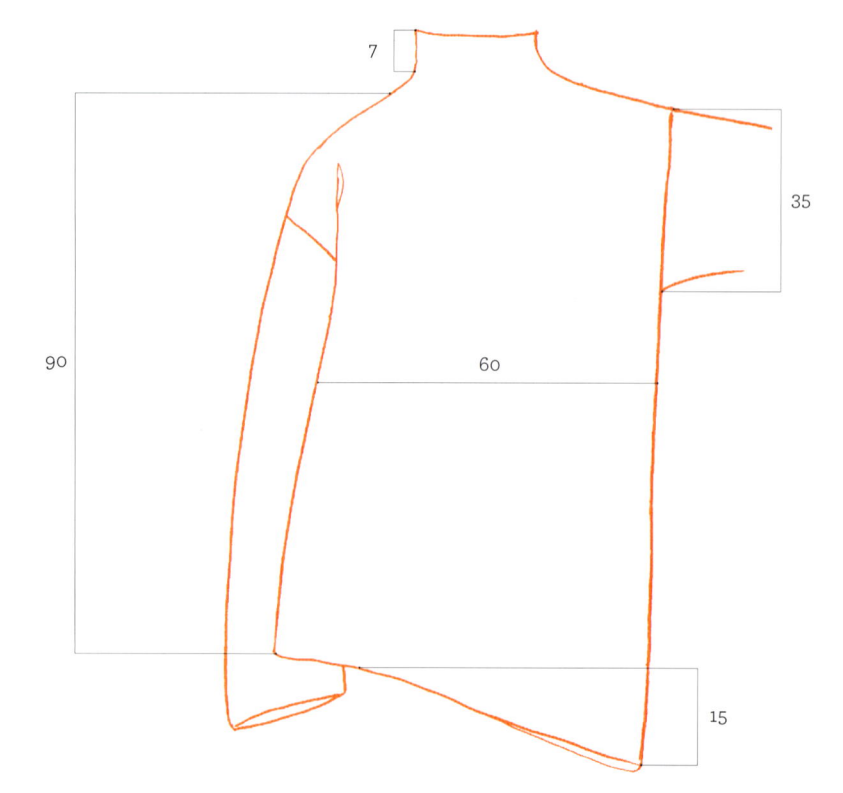

Tapered garment in 3 gg, with cable in the centre.

7

35

90

60

15

80 KNITWEAR FASHION DESIGN ILLUSTRATED STITCHES AND GARMENTS

The garment is made of a set of two types of cable figures with a wave movement in the centre, which combines crossed and plain cables.

ILLUSTRATED STITCHES AND GARMENTS **KNITWEAR FASHION DESIGN**

CABLE
+ LINKS

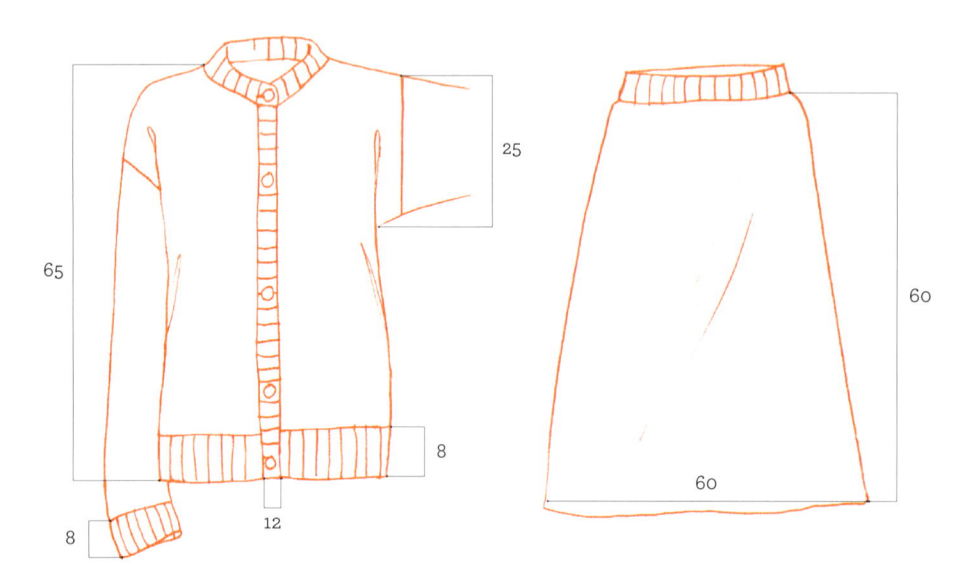

Two-piece suit. The cardigan, with round neck open at the front goes with a bell-shaped skirt in the same knit.

82 **KNITWEAR FASHION DESIGN** ILLUSTRATED STITCHES AND GARMENTS

The design is a very interesting set of figure eight and chessboard pattern of squares in links. The result is a close knit in 5 gg with an ideal texture for this type of very innovative garment.

DOUBLE CABLES

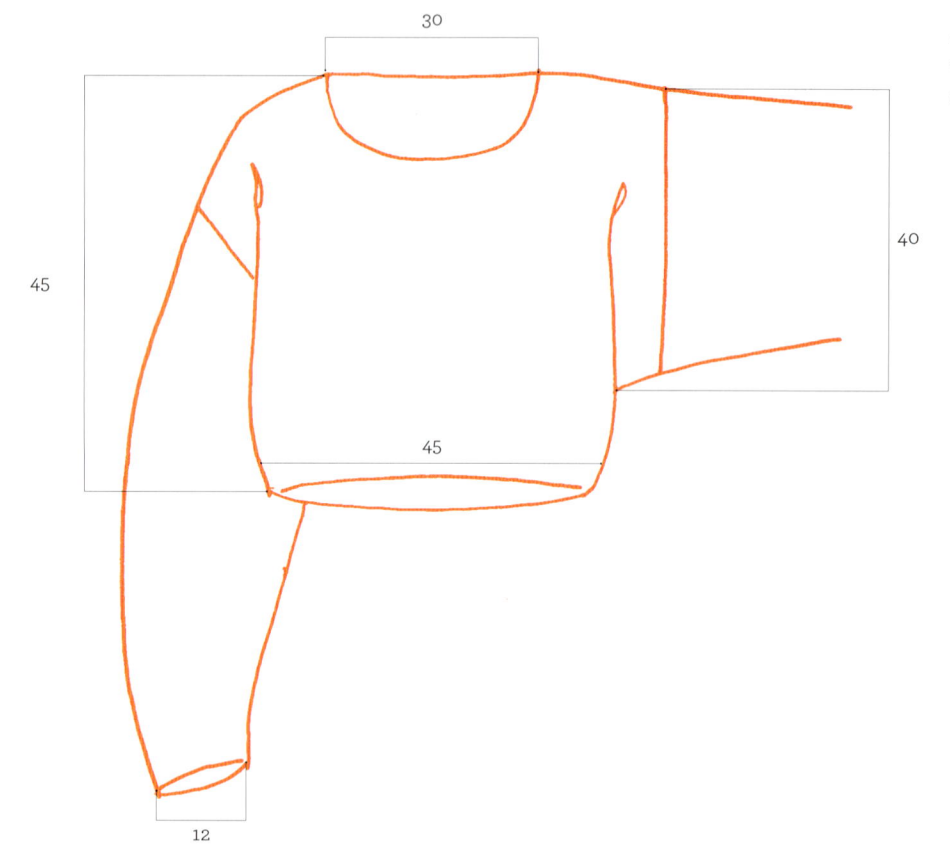

Short loose-fitting garment that skims the waist and has extra large sleeves, giving it a contemporary look.

84 **KNITWEAR FASHION DESIGN** ILLUSTRATED STITCHES AND GARMENTS

Double cables are always made by crossing stitches, and the many possibilities they offer make it possible to obtain highly varied effects.

CABLE

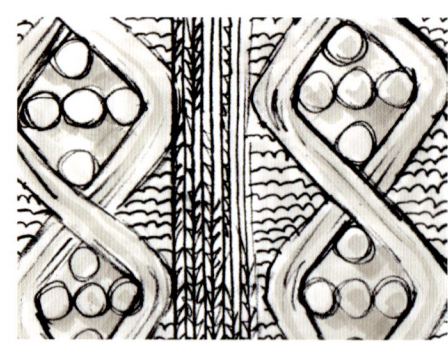

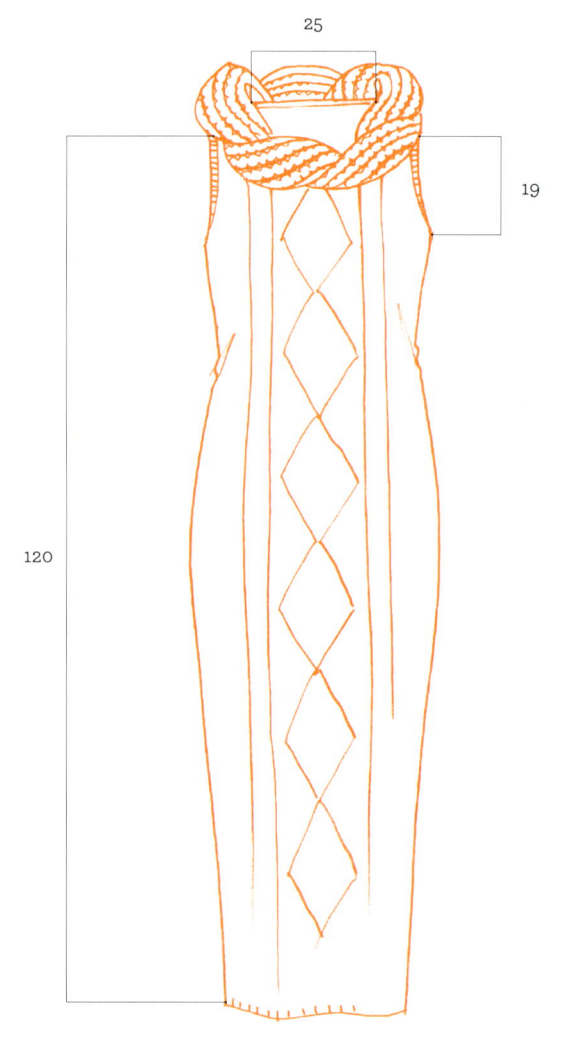

25

19

120

Tight-fitting sleeveless dress, designed to be worn with other garments to create a layered look.

86 KNITWEAR FASHION DESIGN ILLUSTRATED STITCHES AND GARMENTS

Long, fitted, sleeveless dress, knitted in 5 gg. The neck is made from strips of twisted mini cables, to give the pattern a more original touch. It is knitted with crossed diamonds with hazelnut-type raised circles in the centre of the garment, and links in the background. The garment is knitted in plain wool-look yarn.

ILLUSTRATED STITCHES AND GARMENTS **KNITWEAR FASHION DESIGN** 87

GEOMETRIC OPENWORK

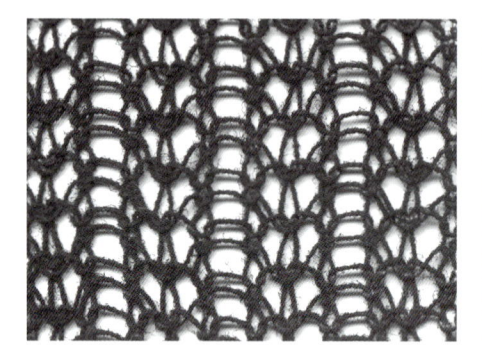

Skirt with 2x2 ribs on the hips to better gather the shape.

15

55

88 **KNITWEAR FASHION DESIGN** ILLUSTRATED STITCHES AND GARMENTS

This openwork is in 3 gg, has large holes, is almost transparent, and is in a cotton-like round yarn. It is a stitch that is well-suited to simple garments with a loose-fitting design, such as those worn over other clothes, and particularly ideal for the layered look currently in vogue. The skirt is knee-length and gathered.

FRINGES

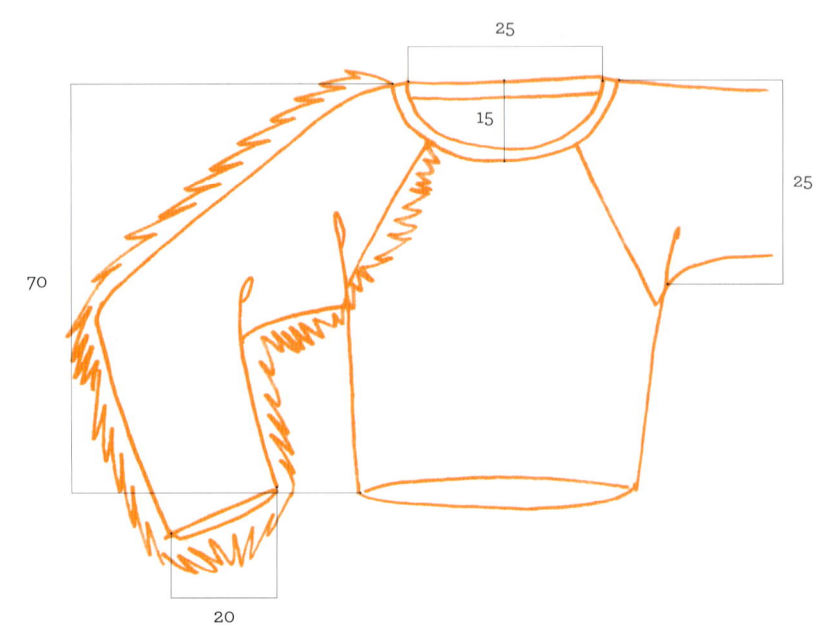

The contrast is the most important thing in this garment, a crop sweater with long fringed sleeves.

90 KNITWEAR FASHION DESIGN ILLUSTRATED STITCHES AND GARMENTS

This is a combination of fringes in plain and reverse (purl) stitch in 3 gg. The front and back are in plain and reverse (purl) stitch, whilst the sleeves are made in round yarn, to which the fringes have been added by hand. It has very small trims. The garment is made in round yarn and the fringes in wicking yarn, both in the same plain colour.

RIB

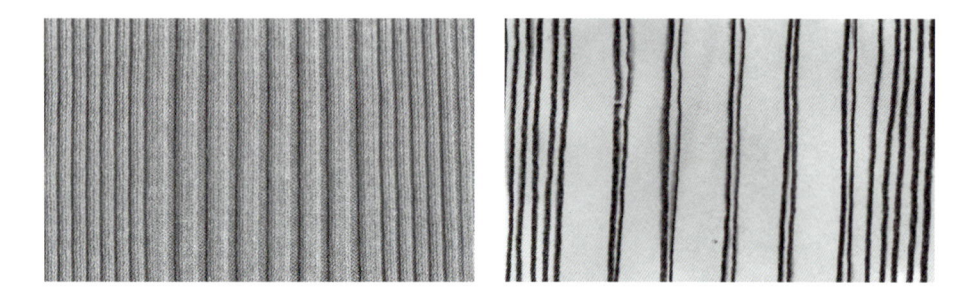

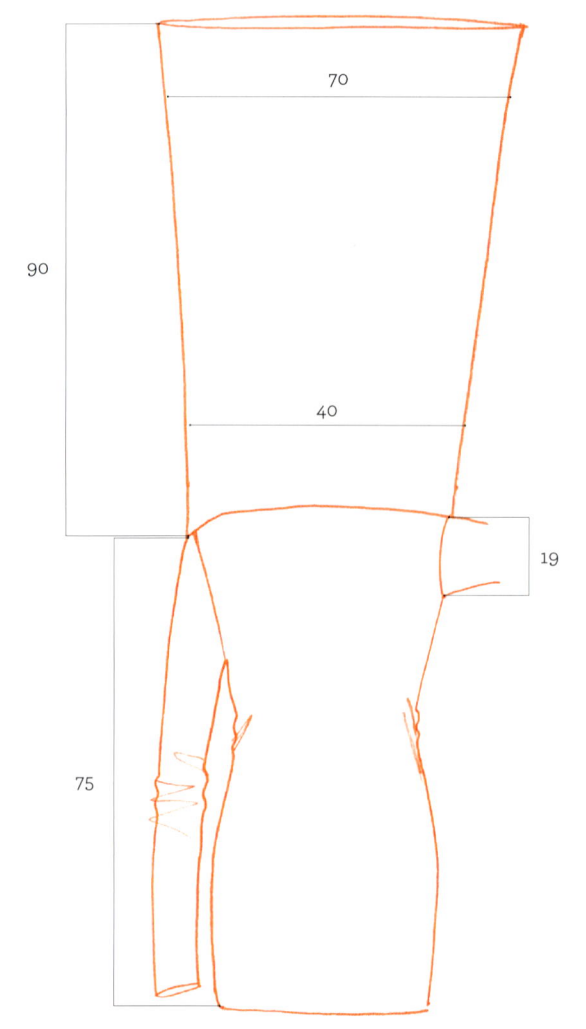

Tight-fitting mini dress, with the innovative detail of a large roll-neck which contrasts with the rest of the garment.

70

90

40

19

75

92 KNITWEAR FASHION DESIGN ILLUSTRATED STITCHES AND GARMENTS

Ribs are stretchy and reversible, and are used to finish off a garment, to make the borders on the hems and cuffs, or for making facings and necks. The rib shown here is a set of two sizes: 4x4 and 2x2, in 10 gg and round yarn.

FALSE RIB

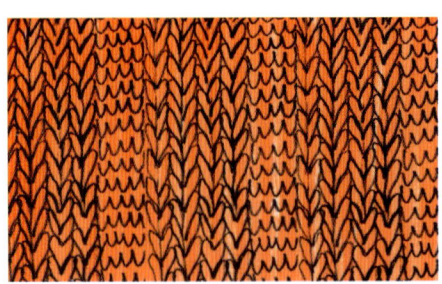

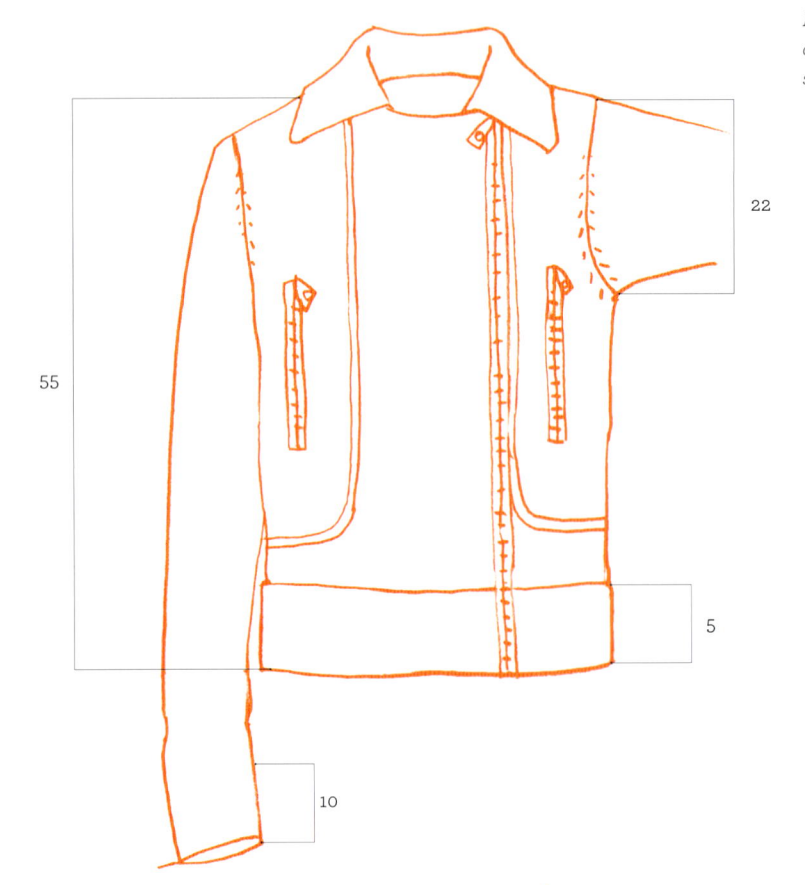

Biker-style jacket, knitted in 5 gg stitch. It has a roll-neck, side zip opening and pockets with side zips.

22

55

5

10

94 KNITWEAR FASHION DESIGN ILLUSTRATED STITCHES AND GARMENTS

These ribs appear normal from the front, but behind, by using all the needles, the ribs are flat and not drawn together; there is no shrinking or gathering. This is useful when making a biker-style jacket, a classic leather garment, as it allows for the knitted fabric to be cut as if it were knitted flat. With the help of the stitch, this basic has been revamped in a new way. The false ribs are in 5 gg; however they can be knitted in any gauge and yarn.

ROMANTIC-STYLE OPENWORK

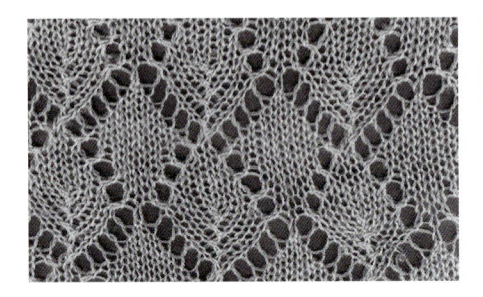

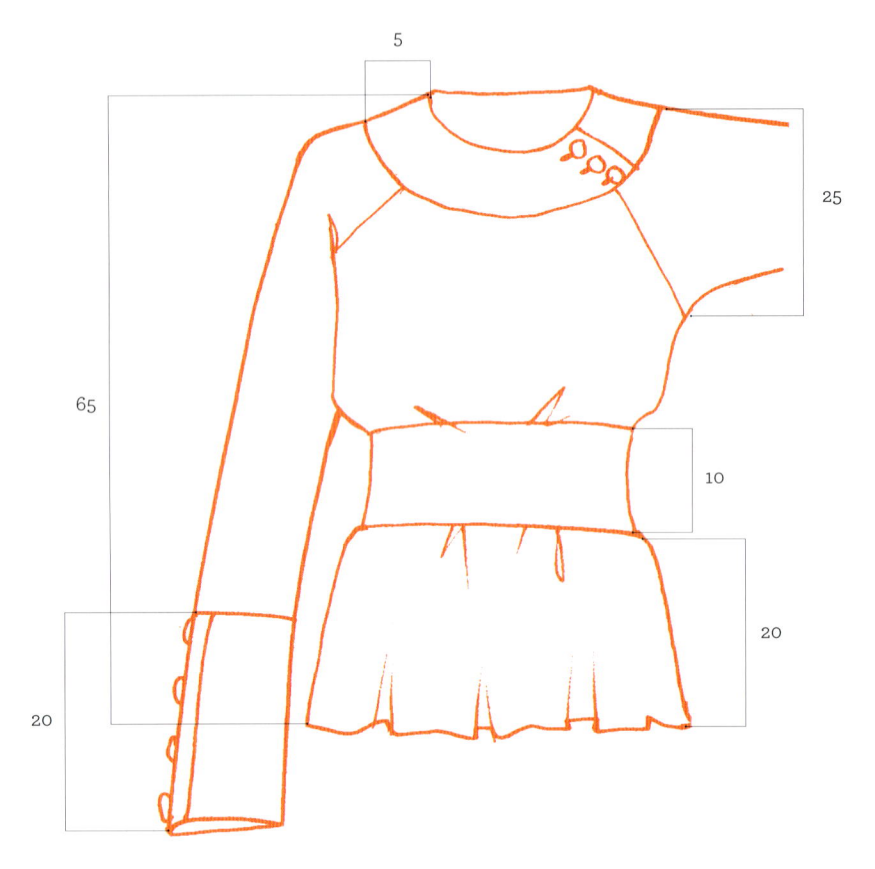

Loose round-neck sweater. The wide ribs gather at the waist. The cuffs are very wide and loose with side buttoning. There is a wide band at the neckline with vertical ribbing.

5

25

65

10

20

20

96 KNITWEAR FASHION DESIGN   ILLUSTRATED STITCHES AND GARMENTS

Romantic-style openwork is made in 5 gg in wool and mohair yarn. This type of openwork can be done in various yarns with a cotton, silk or wool-like appearance, but it is always better to use a yarn with a smooth round structure without too many added fancy elements. The design of the garment is based on the 1960s, a very contemporary look which perfectly suits this style of stitch

OPENWORK

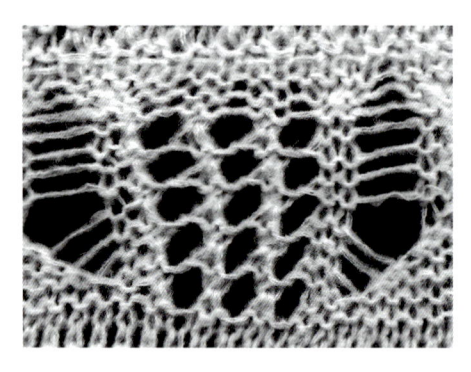

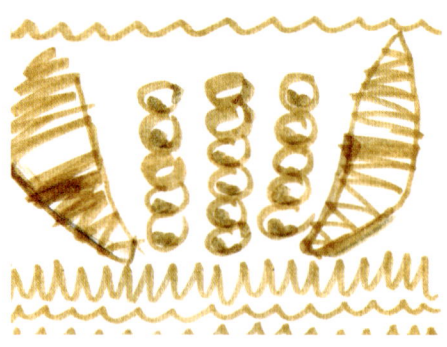

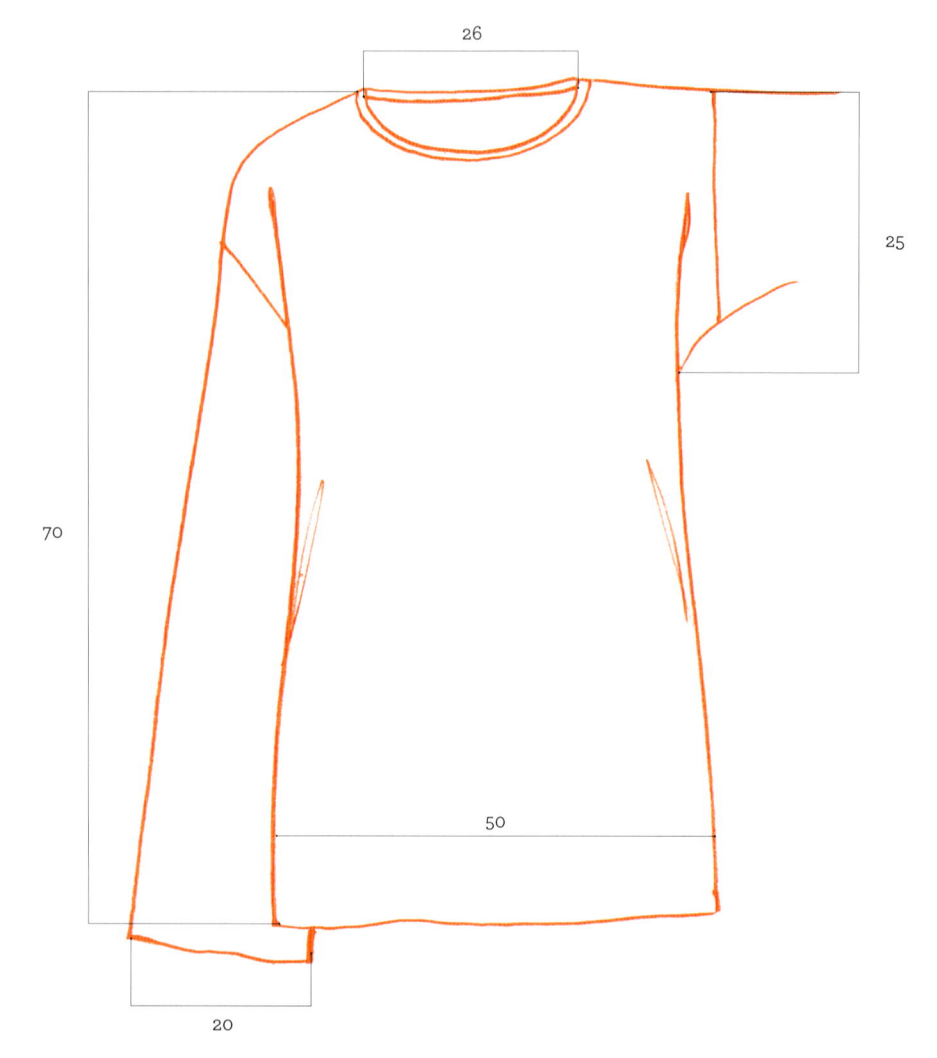

This is a basic loose-fitting garment with tapered cuffs and mini ribs on the trims.

26

25

70

50

20

98 **KNITWEAR FASHION DESIGN** ILLUSTRATED STITCHES AND GARMENTS

There are many different types of openwork including fancy, geometric, drop stitch and lace. The stitch is worked in all types and thicknesses of yarn. The design of the garment is based on different sized openings and the creativity lies in the loose yarns which give an original appearance to the openwork. It is in 5 gg and yarn with a mohair look.

HOLES + FLOATING YARNS

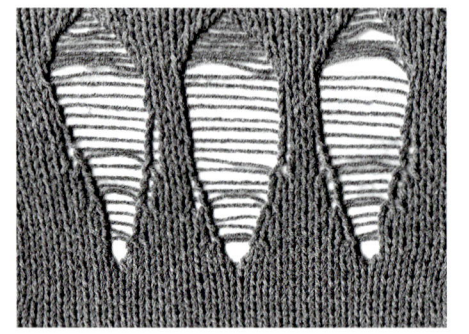

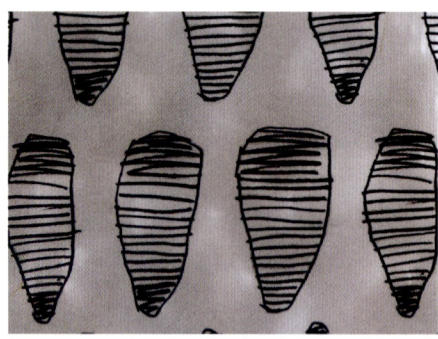

Loose straight waist-length tunic, with drop shoulders and high round neck.

This stitch has a ripped feel which allows for the inside to be visible due to the floating yarns. This knit is used for garments designed to be worn on top of other clothes, allowing for colours and different materials to be played with. For these stitches to be shown off to their best advantage they should be knitted in heavy gauges, 3 gg and 5 gg. However, the yarns can vary, from cottons to wools including fancy yarns such as knotted, tweeds, slubs, bouclé, or napped; in fact almost any yarn can be used. Ideally the garments should be simple so that the design of the stitch can be better appreciated.

JACQUARD

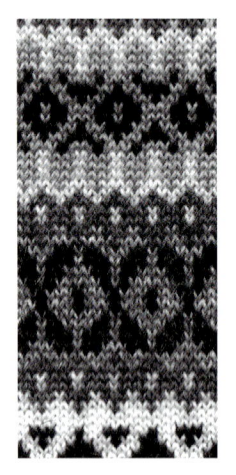

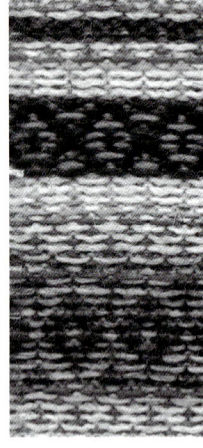

Short sweater, with high round neck and long cuffs.

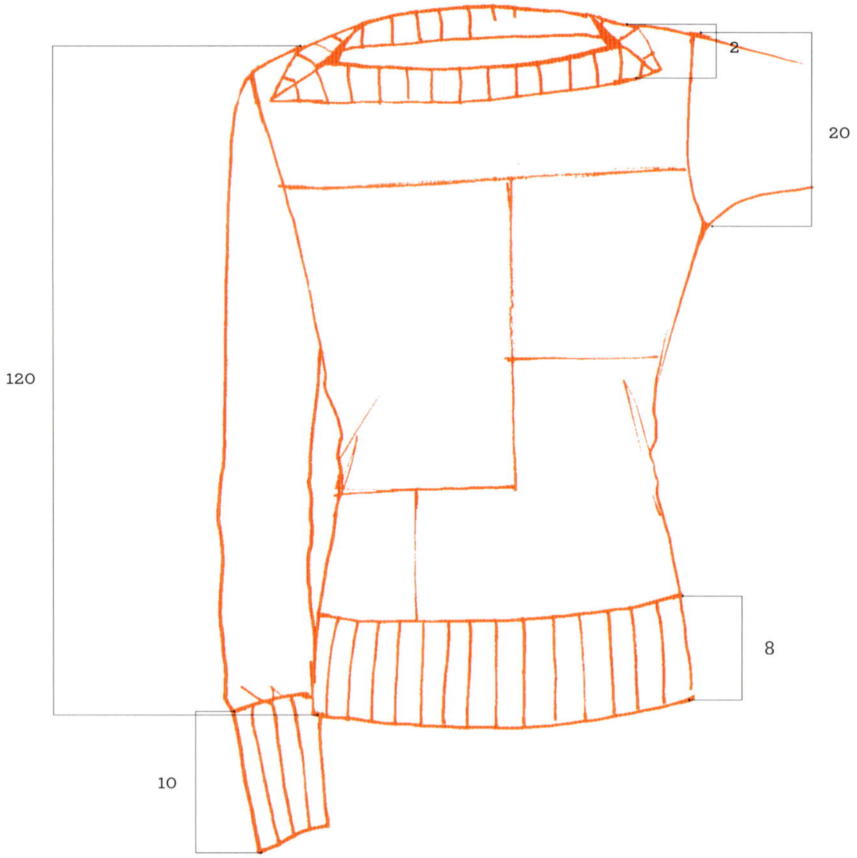

120

20

2

8

10

102 **KNITWEAR FASHION DESIGN** ILLUSTRATED STITCHES AND GARMENTS

Jacquard is a technique that can be used to design practically anything: geometric, figurative or floral designs; large or small patterns and models in any combination of colours and yarns. It is also suitable for any gauge. Jacquard, in some cases, leaves the loose ends behind the design and some designers use them by putting them at the front, as is the case in part of the design shown here. This jacquard design takes its inspiration from the traditional English style and is made up of various materials in a patchwork where the lines and the jacquard of the front and the back are combined.

DOUBLE KNIT

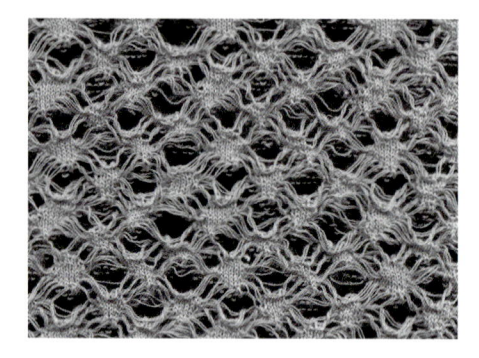

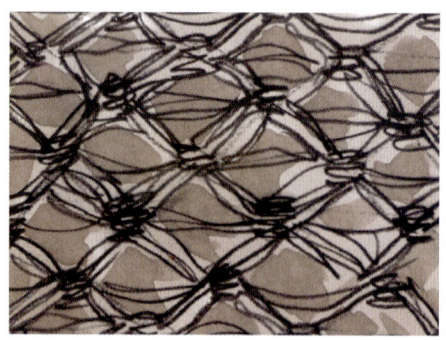

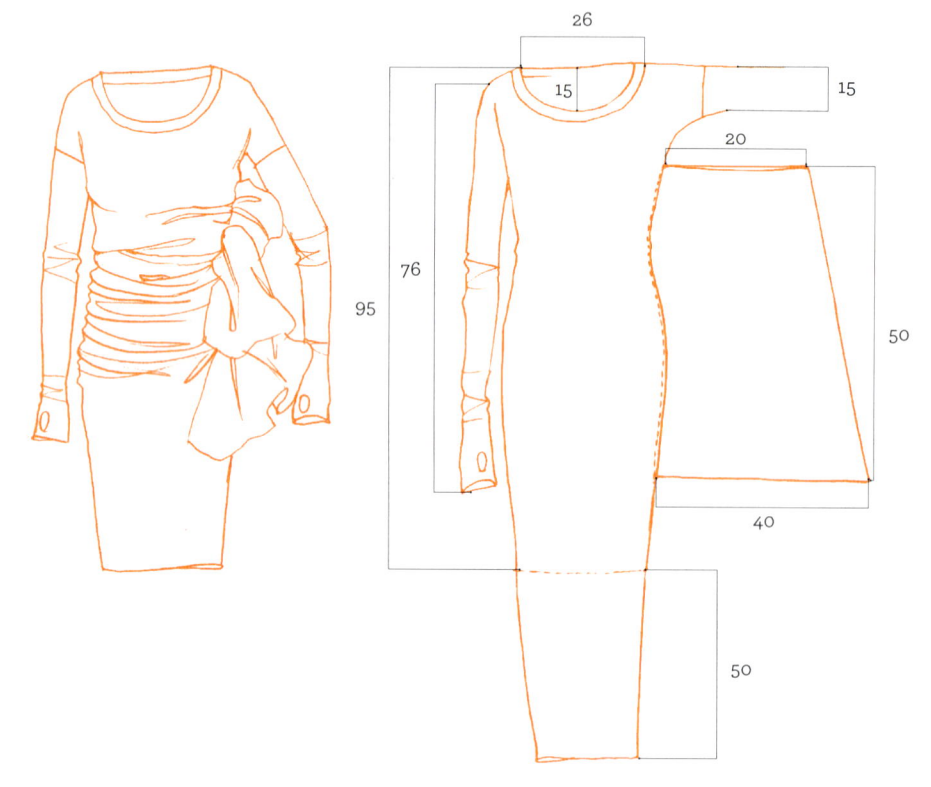

Straight knee-length dress, with draping in the centre and gathered at the side. It has a low round neck and narrow armholes making the sleeves very tight-fitting so as to show off the draping and ruches to their best advantage.

104　KNITWEAR FASHION DESIGN　ILLUSTRATED STITCHES AND GARMENTS

Two parts are worked on with this stitch: the plain stitch which goes behind, in a different colour to that at the front, and the stitch at the front that forms, by virtue of holes and floating ends, a structure through which the knit and inside colour are visible. Two yarns and different colours can be blended, and the gauges can vary between 5 gg and 12 gg. The untidy appearance of the knit, together with the combination of colours, gives it a fresh look. The garment is a casual dress, whose originality lies in the central draping which is gathered unevenly at the side.

RAISED PATTERNS

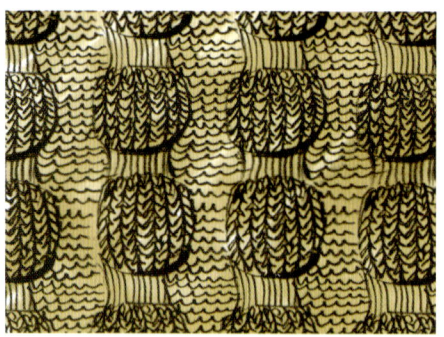

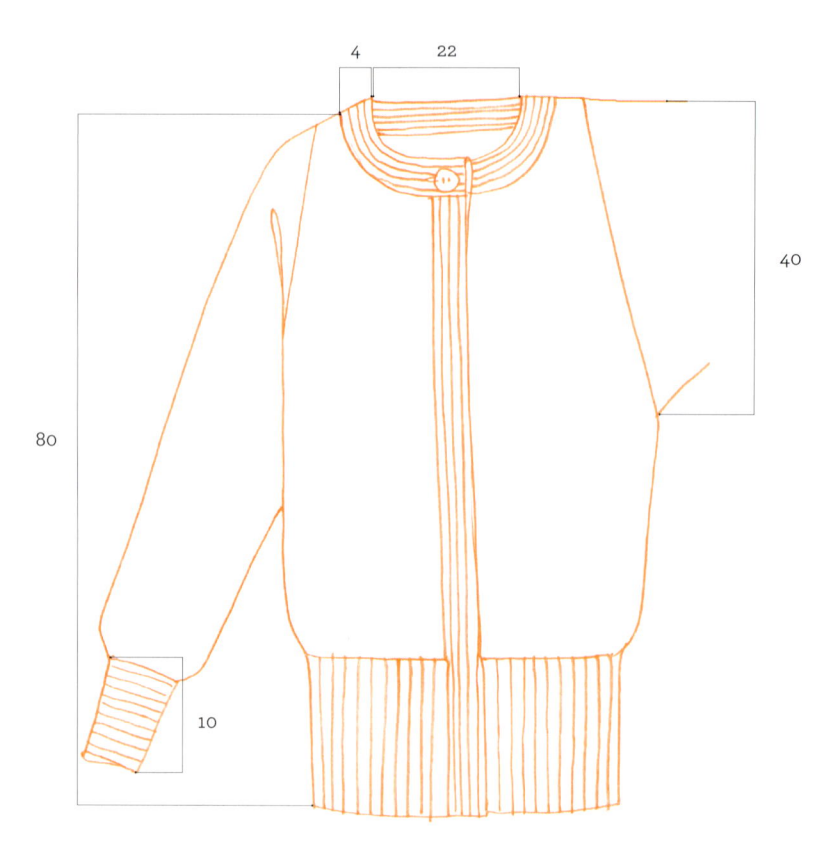

Loose cardigan with wide ribbing (4x2) at the hem. The lapel and the cuffs are knitted in vertical rib (2x1). The buttons are hidden, except for the one at the top, on a strip of the same vertical rib which finishes off the deep round neck. The sleeves, which are in a deep raglan style, give volume and shape to the garment.

106 KNITWEAR FASHION DESIGN   ILLUSTRATED STITCHES AND GARMENTS

The design of stitches with raised patterns gives an original finish to a garment. These raised patterns can be of any type, romantic or geometric, and are well-suited to garments with a simple design where the originality lies in the design of the stitch. Shown here are some squares which have been knitted in 5 gg and woollen-look yarn. Stitches with patterns which are raised significantly are better knitted with round yarns, as they give more elasticity to the knit and make the pattern more pronounced.

CROCHET

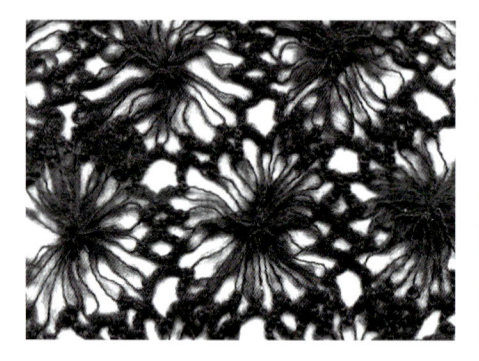

Loose, flowing skirt with gathered elasticated waist.

115

108 **KNITWEAR FASHION DESIGN** ILLUSTRATED STITCHES AND GARMENTS

This hand stitch has been employed to make a design of circular flowers, using a mohair-look yarn which gives it volume yet keeps it lightweight. These lines of crochet stitches are well-suited for making ponchos, shawls or light cardigans in a romantic style and also very contemporary young-looking garments, such as this hippy-style skirt which is long, loose and flowing.

FRILLS

Low round neck jacket with tubular facings. The rectangular piece has a close-knit background with knitted frills added to the front of the garment. The cuffs are finished off with two frills.

110 KNITWEAR FASHION DESIGN ILLUSTRATED STITCHES AND GARMENTS

The frill look is created by cutting in half a machine-knitted piece. These knitted frills, in 5 gg, can be made in different yarns and in various colours. For the design of the garment, some frills have been drawn in a semi-transparent material on a close opaque background, all in one colour.

ILLUSTRATED STITCHES AND GARMENTS **KNITWEAR FASHION DESIGN**

CROSSED STRIPS

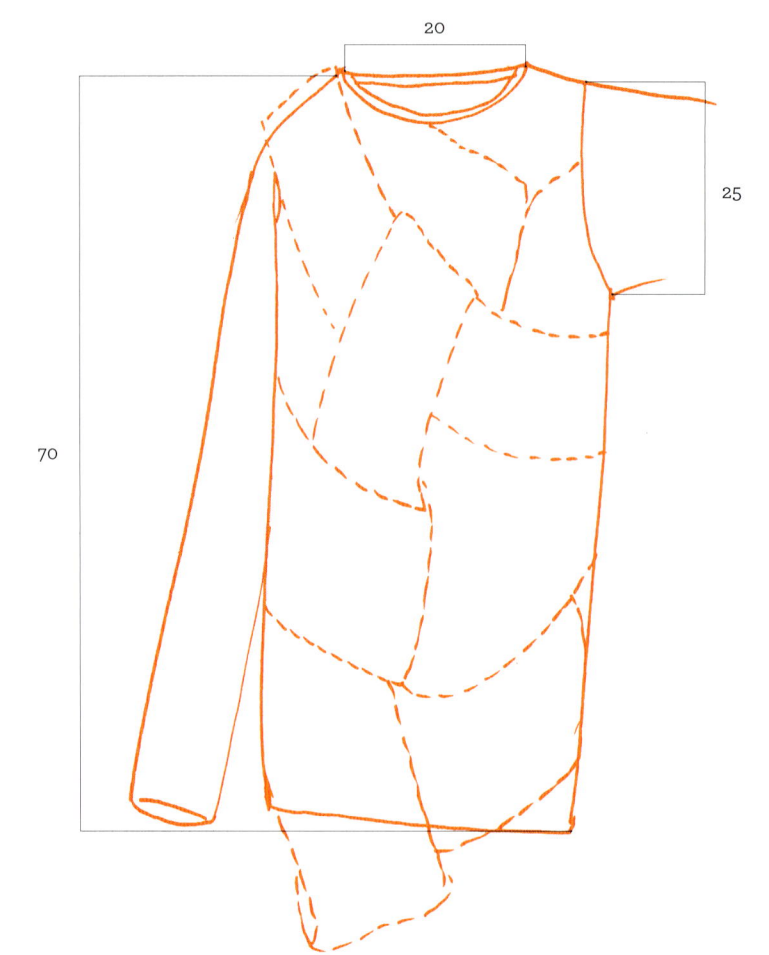

The garment is loose at the hips with a high boat neck joined to the shoulders.

20

25

70

112 **KNITWEAR FASHION DESIGN** ILLUSTRATED STITCHES AND GARMENTS

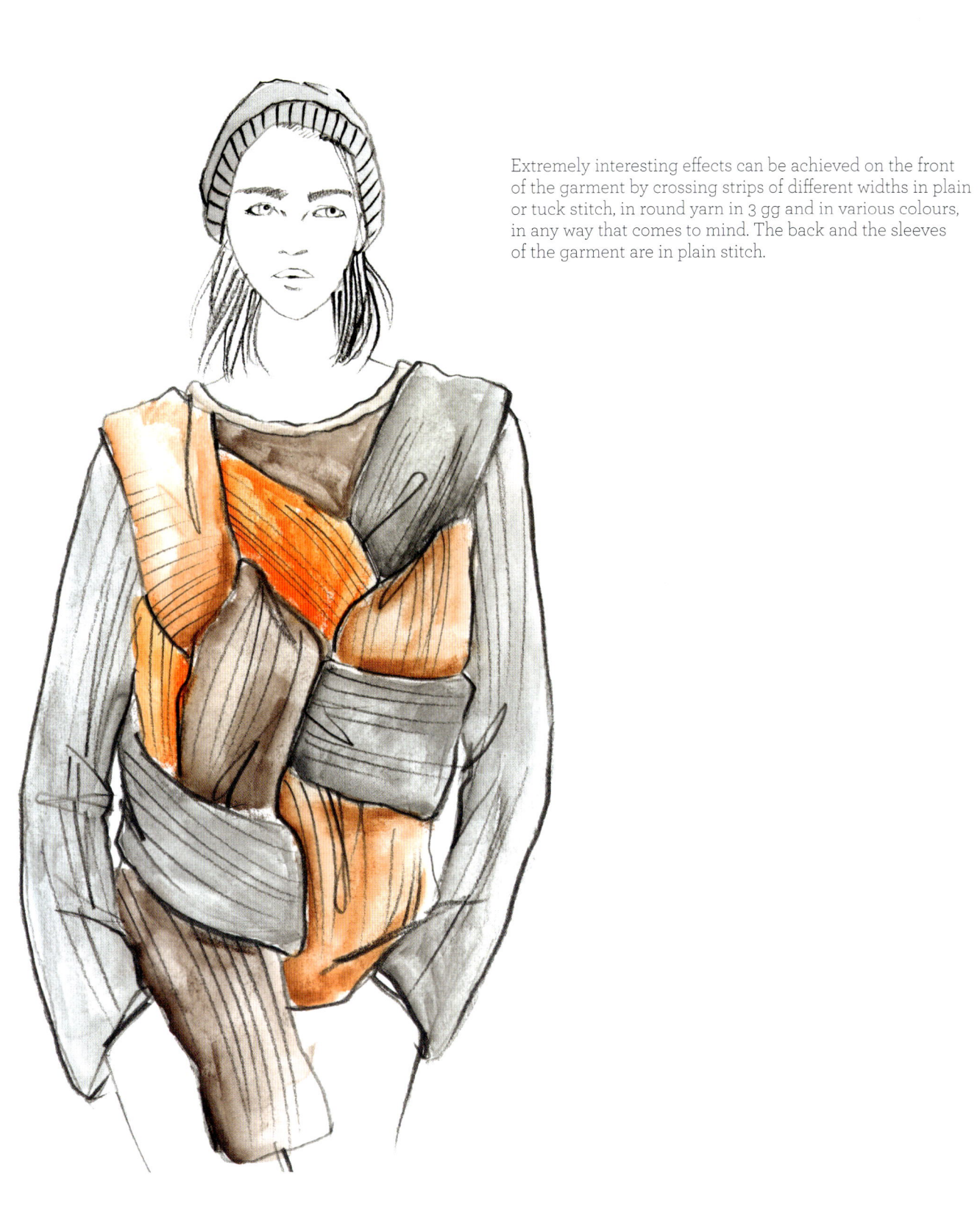

Extremely interesting effects can be achieved on the front of the garment by crossing strips of different widths in plain or tuck stitch, in round yarn in 3 gg and in various colours, in any way that comes to mind. The back and the sleeves of the garment are in plain stitch.

LINKS

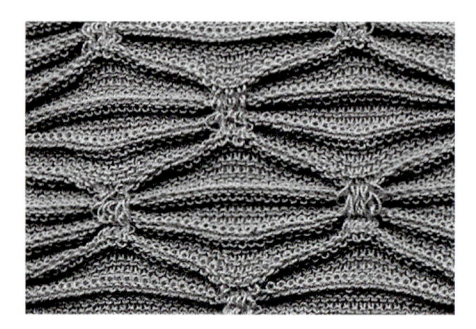

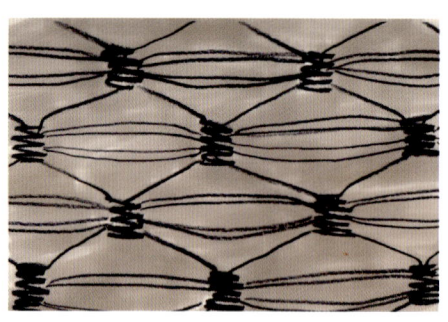

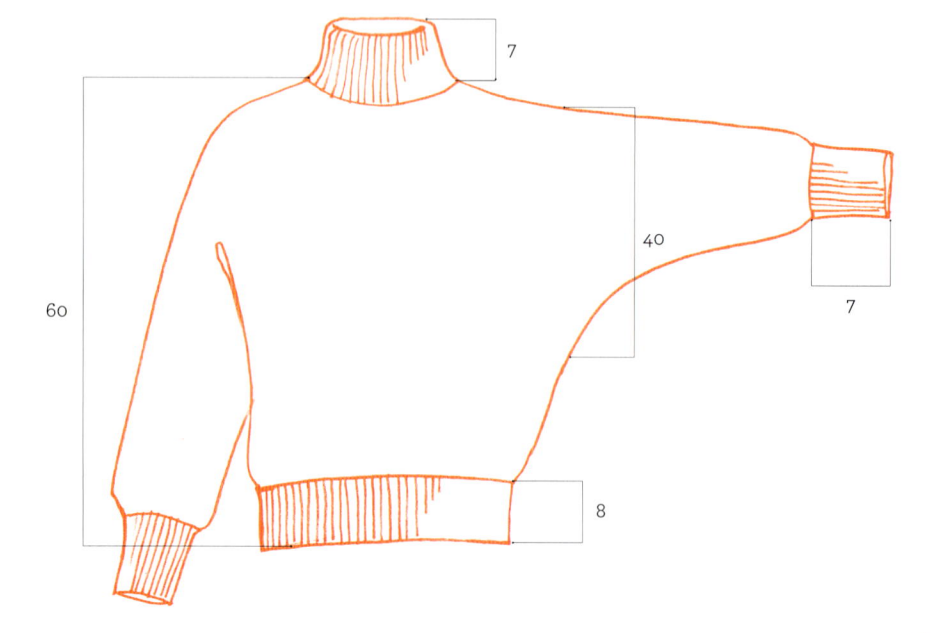

1940s-style retro look sweater with half roll-neck and three-quarter length batwing sleeves.

This is a stitch similar to the back of the plain stitch and can be used to design anything at all, from figurative to floral and geometric patterns. The resulting design can be seen from the front and the back by the way the knit lies. The design shown here is one of elongated diamonds with a gathered knitted fabric and links. It is in a plain round yarn in 8 gg.

ILLUSTRATED STITCHES AND GARMENTS **KNITWEAR FASHION DESIGN** 115

CENTERED LINKS

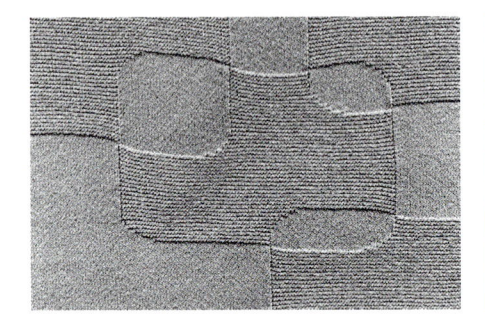

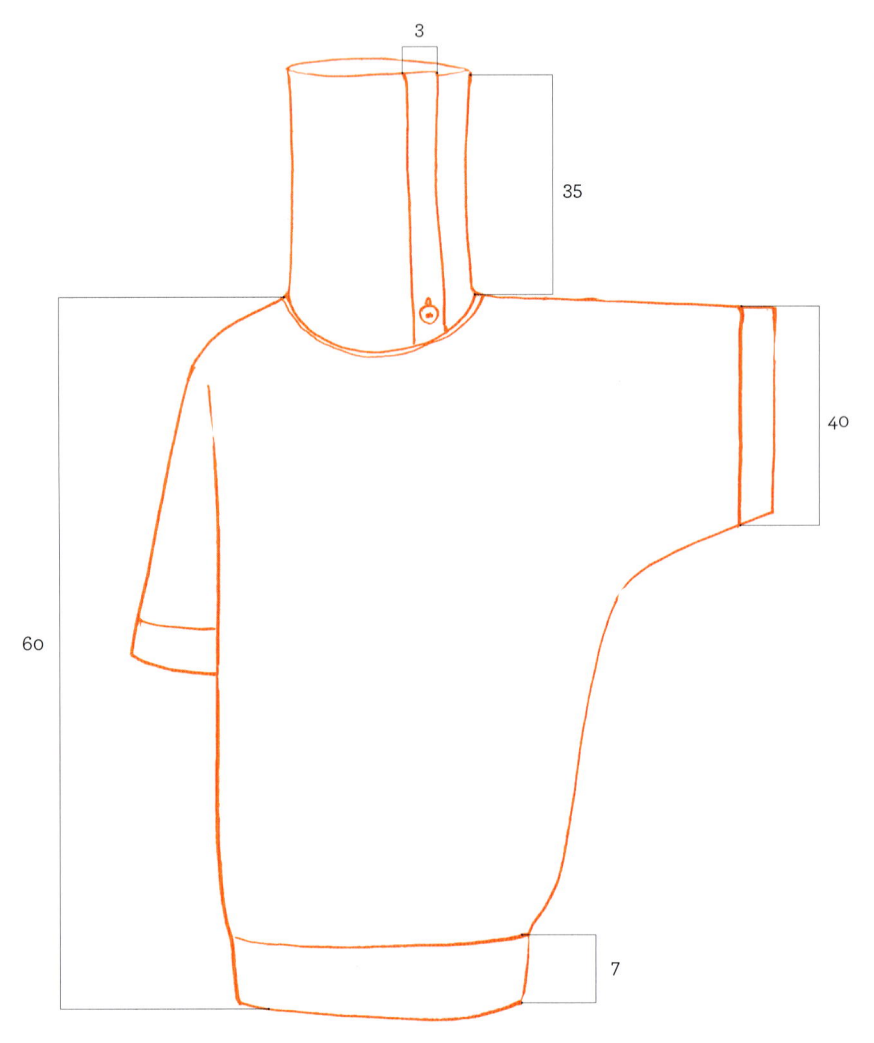

Short loose dress in 3 gg, with an oversize roll-neck and one button at the opening. The elbow-length sleeves are wide and loose. The 4x2 rib of the hem makes it slightly fitted and gives the dress an oval shape.

3

35

40

60

7

116 **KNITWEAR FASHION DESIGN** ILLUSTRATED STITCHES AND GARMENTS

The links technique allows for any design to be traced out, provided it is clean and neat and not elaborate and complicated. It involves making geometric shapes, figurative patterns, stripes and, in general, designs with a very precise look in one colour, with plain round yarns and in any gauge. This garment in 3 gg is notable for the way in which it shows off the connection of the links design on the front.

ILLUSTRATED STITCHES AND GARMENTS **KNITWEAR FASHION DESIGN** 117

ACCESSO-RIES

5

The accessories or finishing of a garment are vitally important. An analysis of a particular season's collections begins by looking in detail at the accessories, before proceeding to study the yarn, texture or colour. The armholes, sleeves, cuffs, facings, neck and neckline, are the details which finish off the garment and give it an original and attractive look. Giving the accessory a different gauge, texture, colour or yarn is just the start of an endless number of ideas that can be found in a collection. The sample shown in this section is a starting point, with the illustrations helping to explain the content. Another essential and equally important factor is being able to illustrate the different thicknesses of gauge. It is essential that the difference between a 3 gg and a 12 gg sweater can be shown with subtle freehand strokes.

ROUND NECK

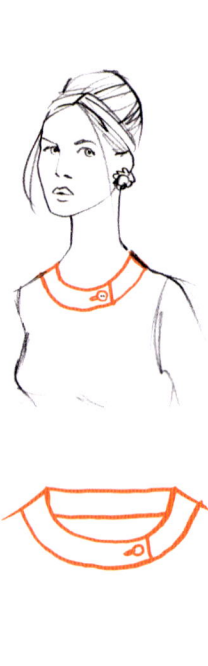

Flat band with button
Sweatshirt
Tubular cut-out band

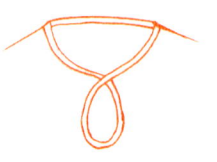

With overhanging facing
Overlock finishing
Low neckline

120　KNITWEAR FASHION DESIGN　ACCESSORIES

V NECK

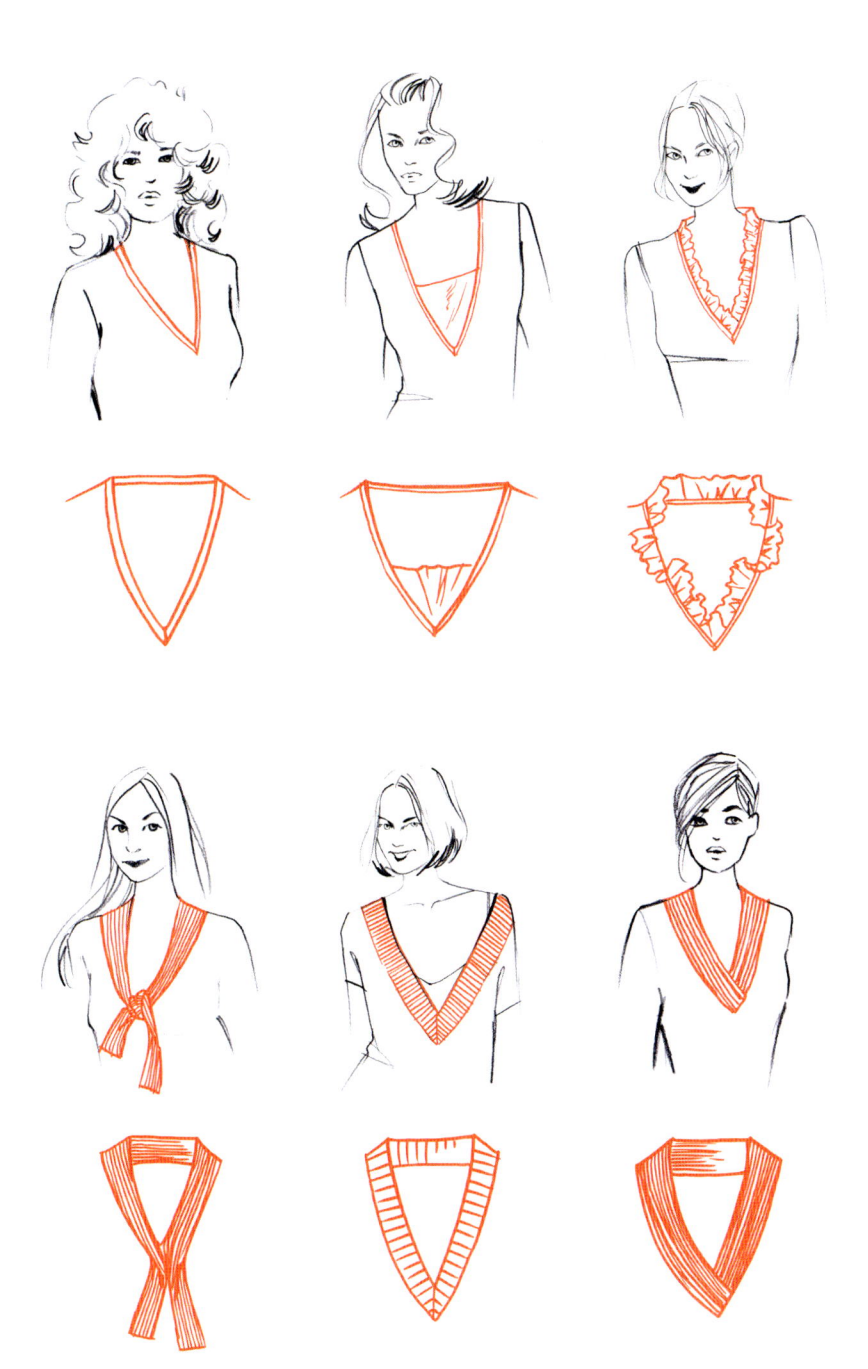

With ribbing
Appliqué
Frills

Loop
Low
Vertical ribbing

ACCESSORIES **KNITWEAR FASHION DESIGN** 121

TURTLENECK

Open roll-neck
Fine gauge
Wide

With zip
Shoulder fastening
Cross-over

122 **KNITWEAR FASHION DESIGN** ACCESSORIES

JACKET COLLARS

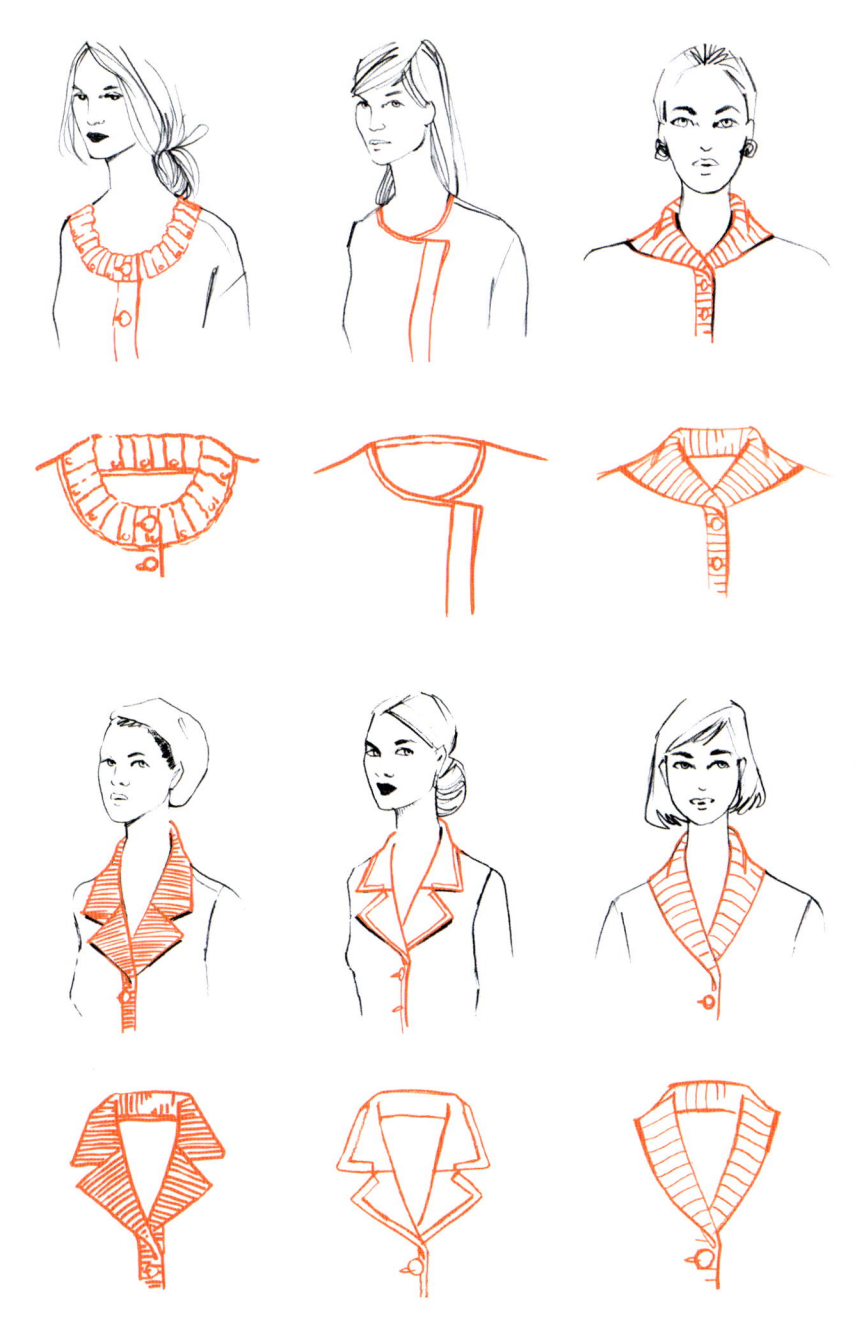

Low-cut round neck
Hidden button-facing
High-neck dinner jacket

Fluted lapel
Tubular lapel
Classic dinner jacket neck

ACCESSORIES **KNITWEAR FASHION DESIGN**

SHIRT COLLARS

Fabric
With cable
Long pile

With zip
Polo neck
Basic

124 KNITWEAR FASHION DESIGN ACCESSORIES

FINISHINGS FOR FACINGS

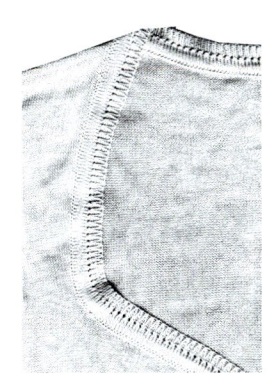

Machine finishing
Flat band
Ribbing + Tubular fine gg

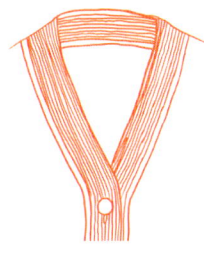

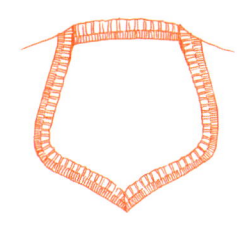

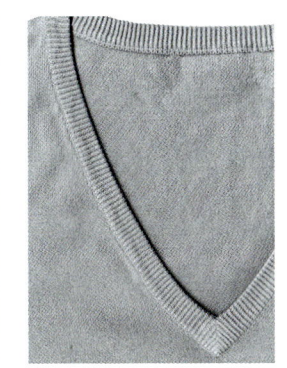

Ribbing 2x2
Coverstitch / Overlock
Ribbing 2x1 fine gg

FINISHINGS FOR FACINGS

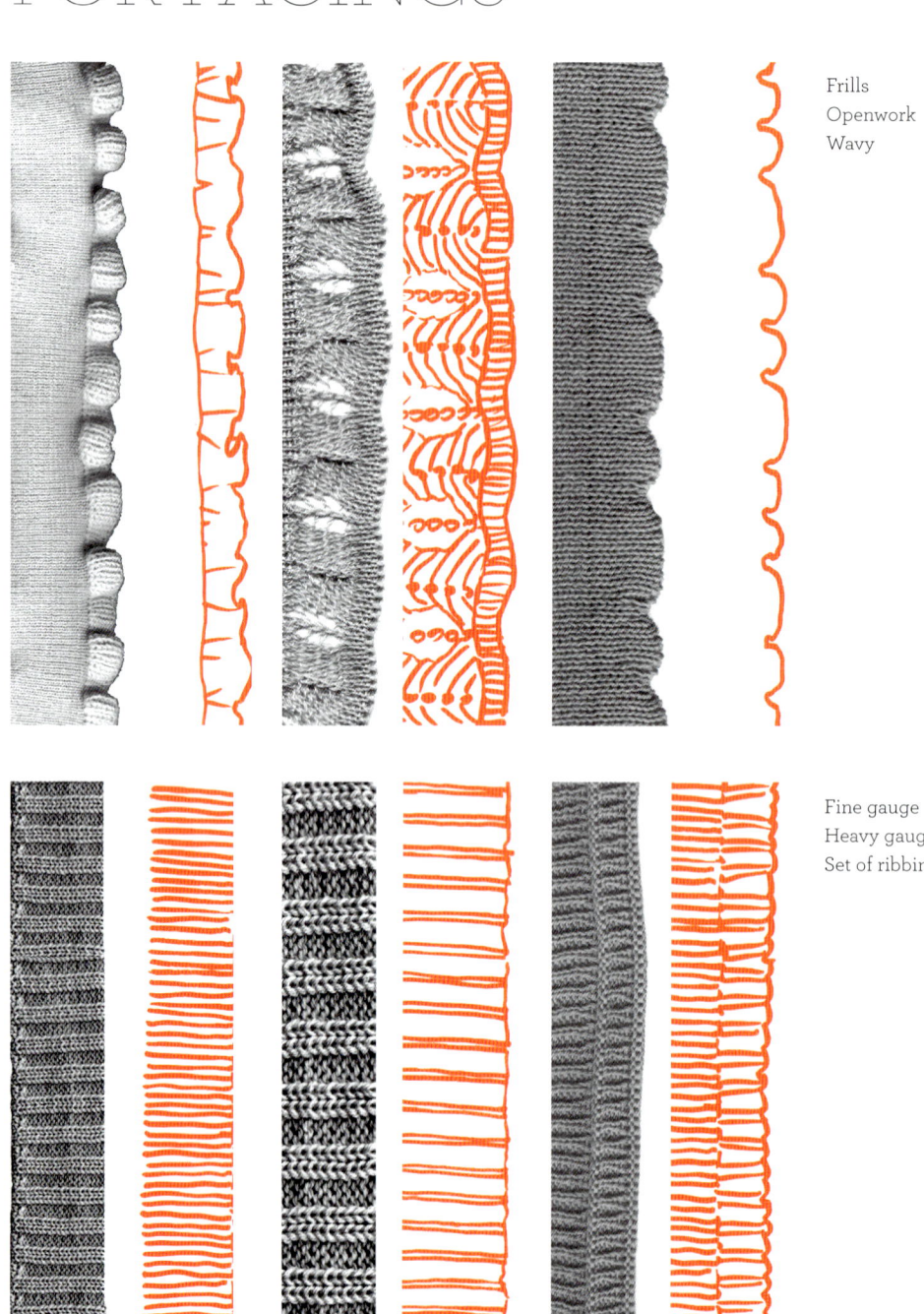

Frills
Openwork
Wavy

Fine gauge
Heavy gauge
Set of ribbing

FINISHINGS FOR FACINGS

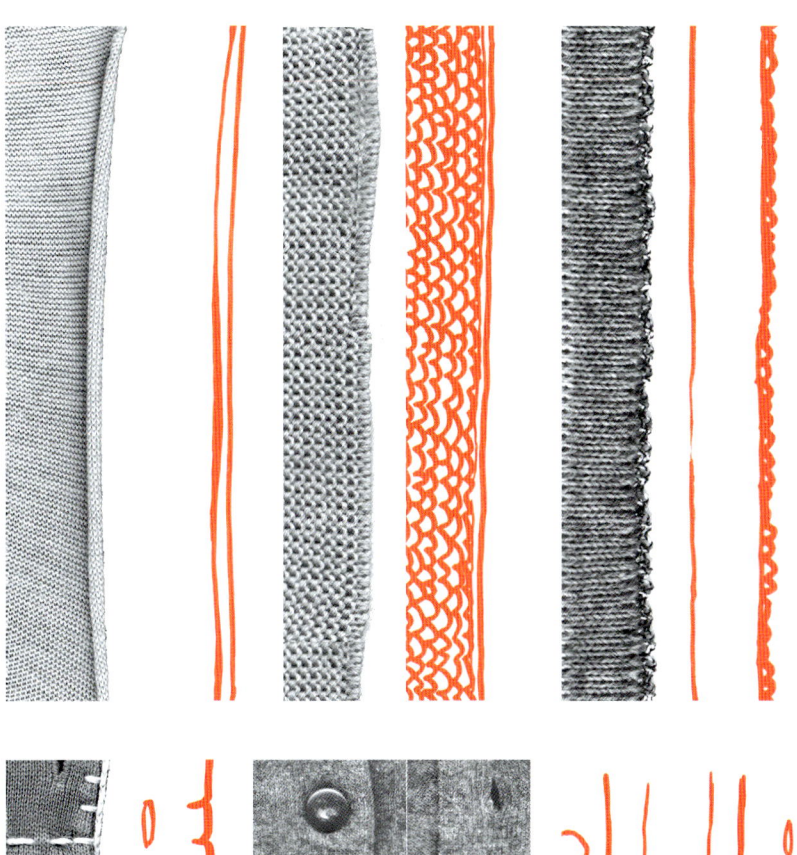

Laser or machine finish
Links
Rib finished off with metallic thread

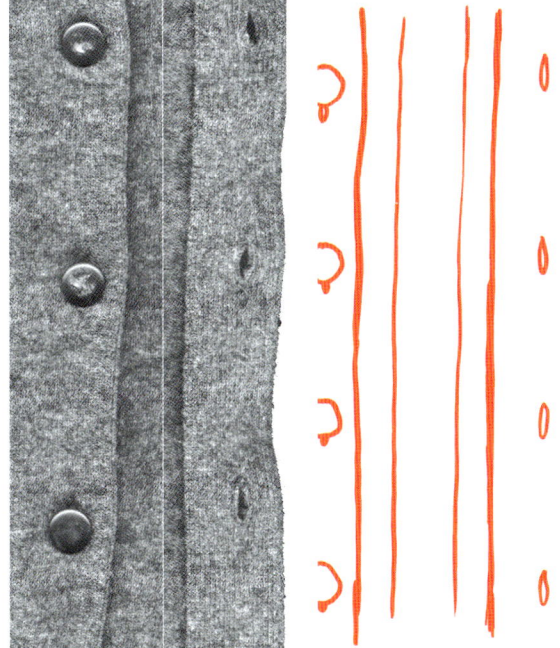

Manual
Flat inside band

ACCESSORIES **KNITWEAR FASHION DESIGN**

CUFFS

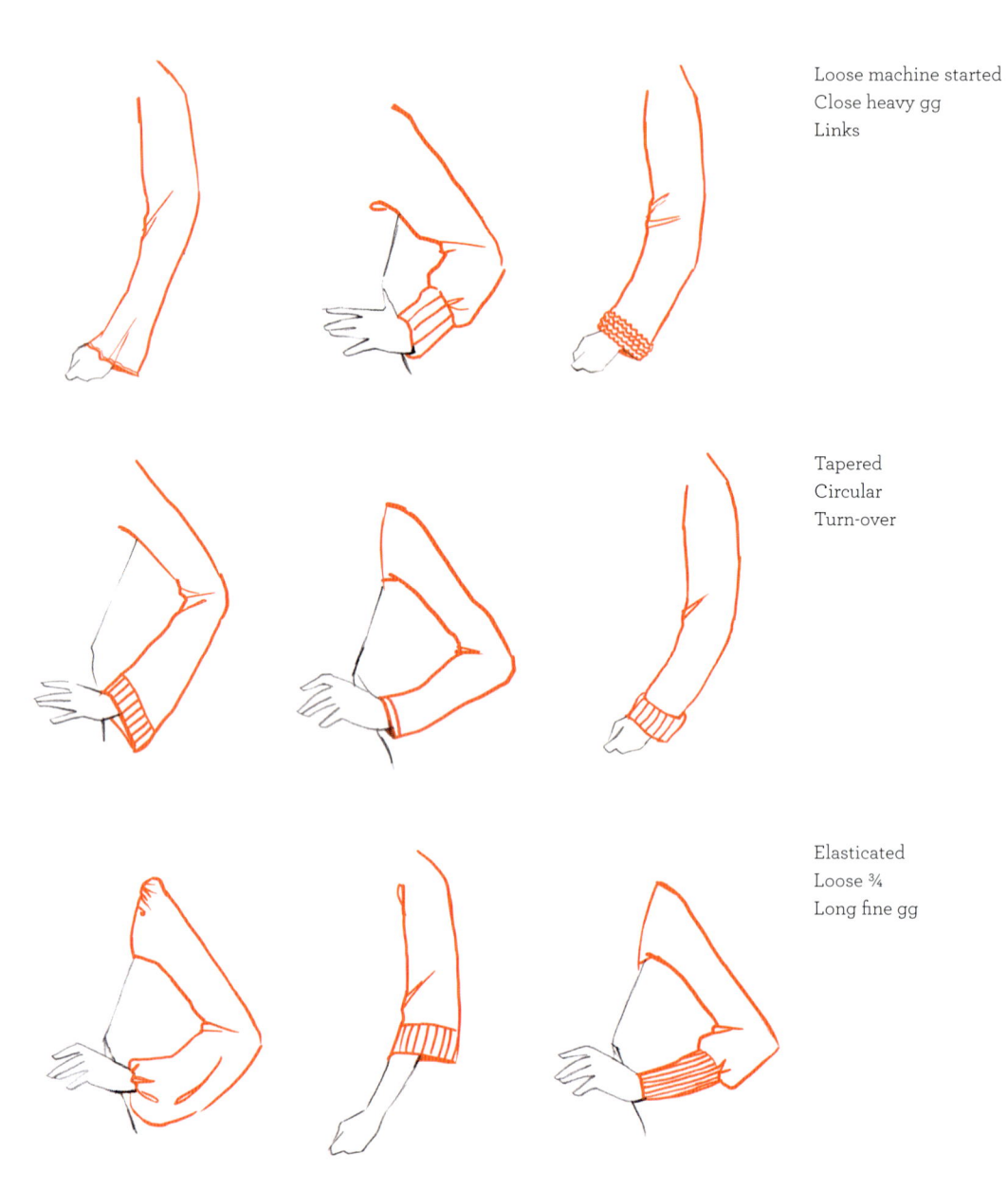

Loose machine started
Close heavy gg
Links

Tapered
Circular
Turn-over

Elasticated
Loose ¾
Long fine gg

FINISHES
FOR HEMS

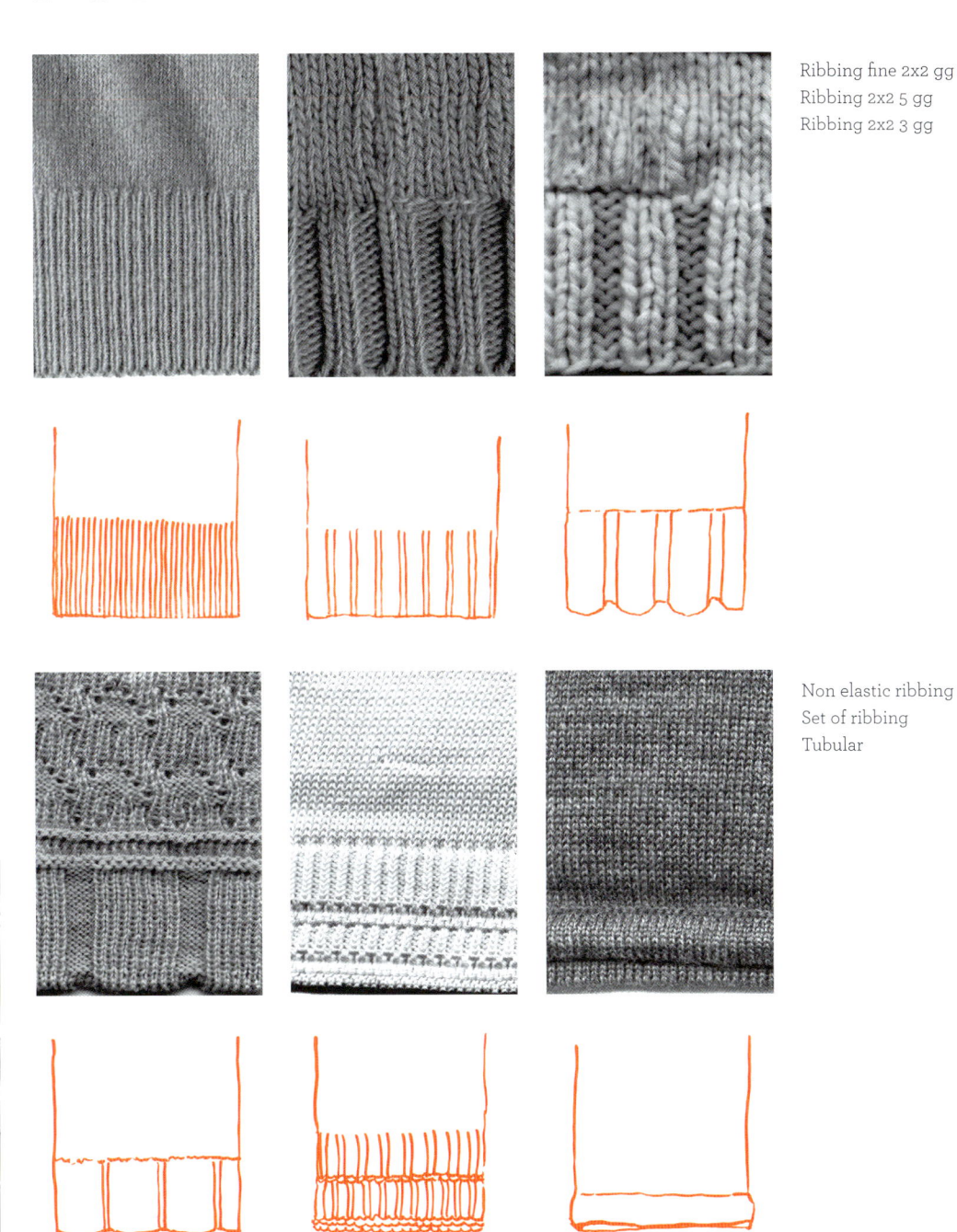

Ribbing fine 2x2 gg
Ribbing 2x2 5 gg
Ribbing 2x2 3 gg

Non elastic ribbing
Set of ribbing
Tubular

ACCESSORIES **KNITWEAR FASHION DESIGN** 129

FINISHES FOR HEMS

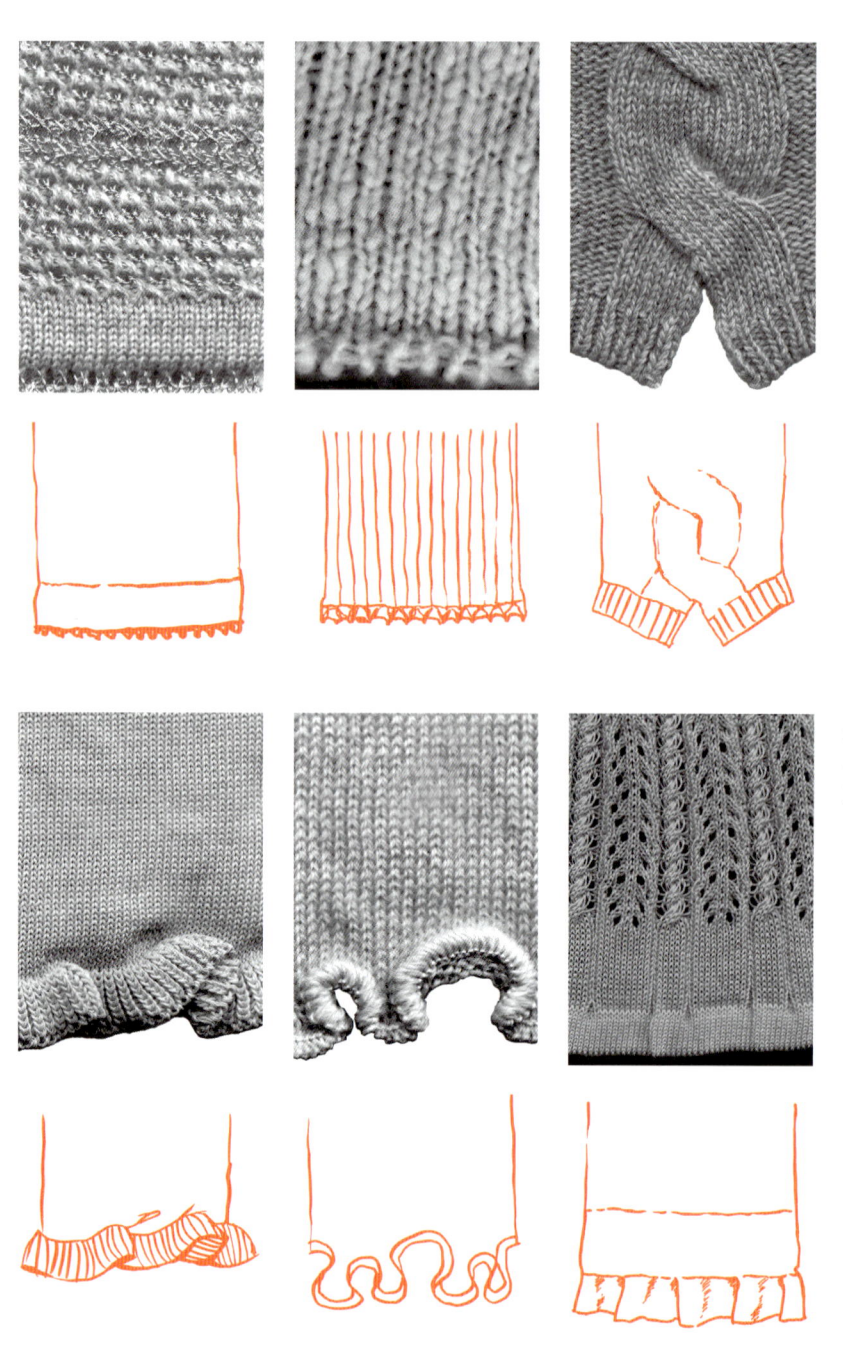

Rib finished off with metallic thread
Started with one layer
With pattern

Frills
Coverstitch
Pleated

130 KNITWEAR FASHION DESIGN ACCESSORIES

FINISHES FOR HEMS

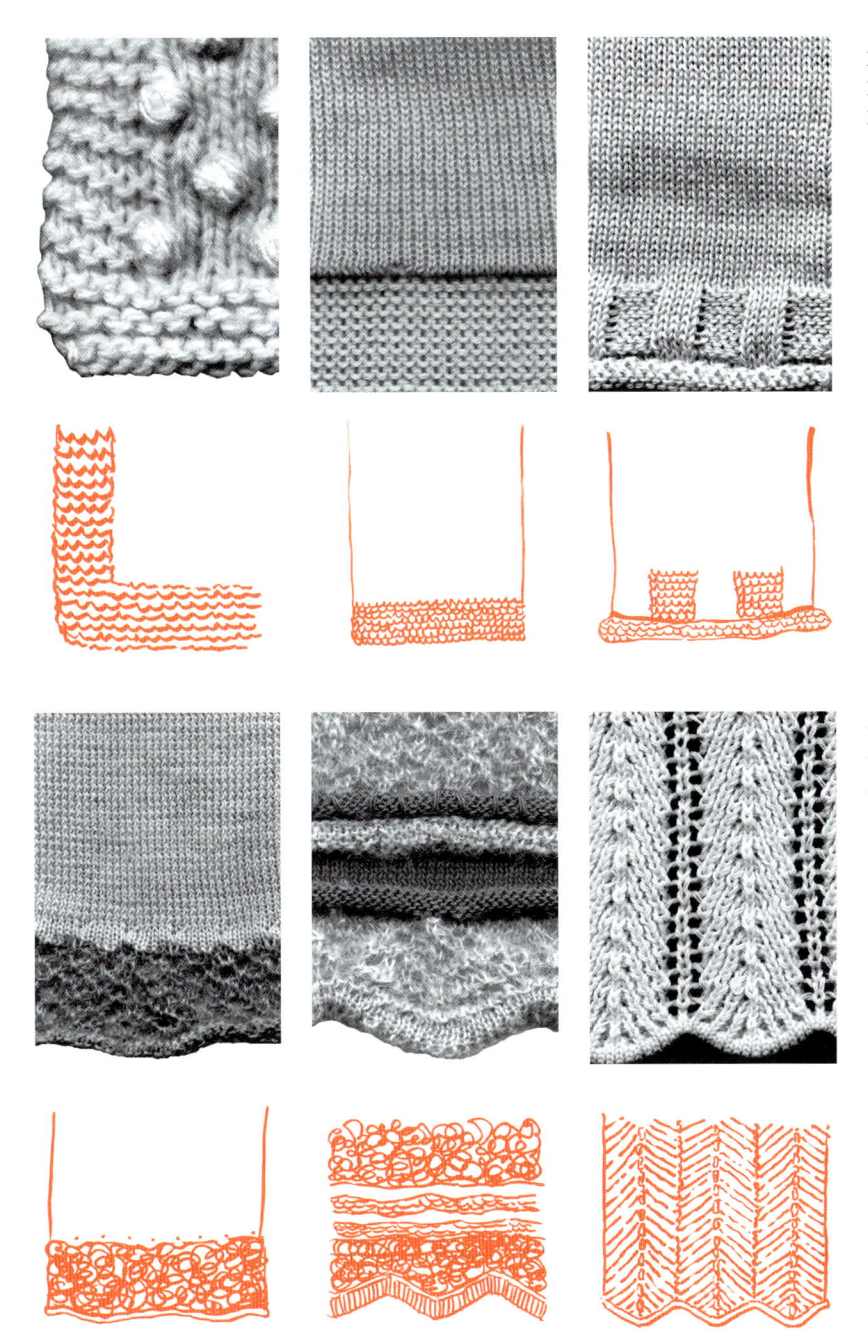

Heavy gg links
Fine gg links
Rolled links

Tuck stitch
Tuck stitch with fine tubular
Openwork

ACCESSORIES **KNITWEAR FASHION DESIGN** 131

HEAVY GAUGES

Heavy gauges are drawn with wide strokes. To show the ribbing, the lines must be thick and have sizeable gaps between them, depending on the thickness of the gauge.

When drawing folds in a piece of knitting in heavy gauge, sketch a few lines sparingly, just those that are essential, and use very light strokes.

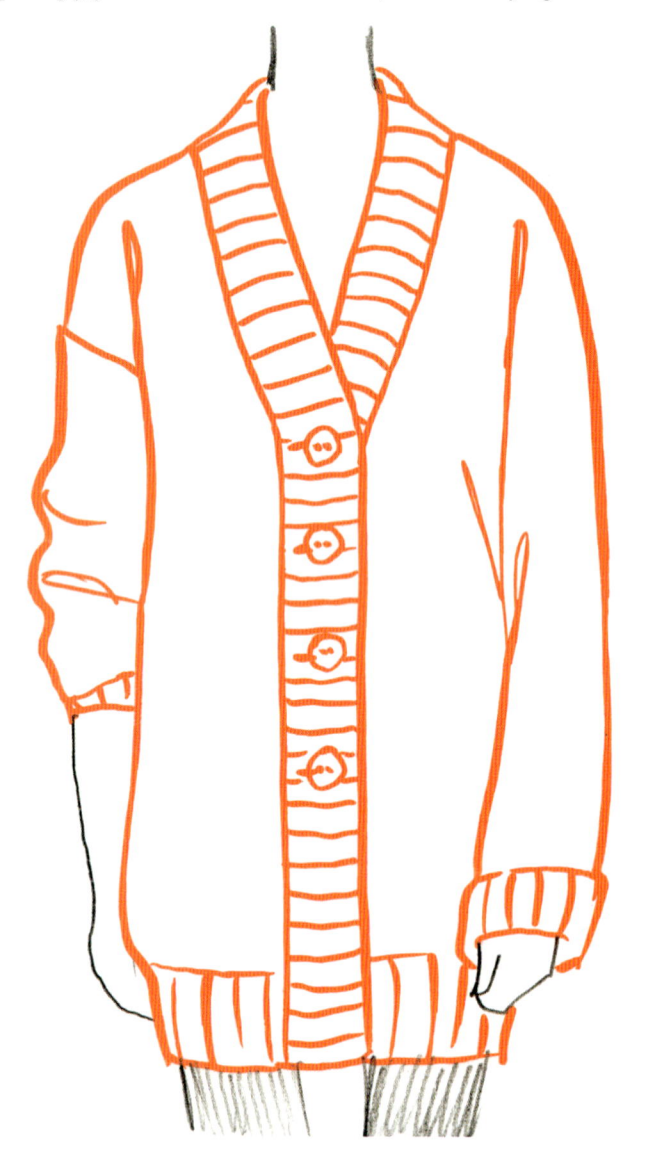

Volume

Roll-neck

V-neck

Cuffs

Hems

132 KNITWEAR FASHION DESIGN ACCESSORIES

FINE GAUGES

Fine gauges are drawn with very light strokes. The lines must be thin and very close to each other to show the ribbing. When drawing folds in a piece of knitting in fine gauge, more lines should be drawn, using very fine flowing strokes.

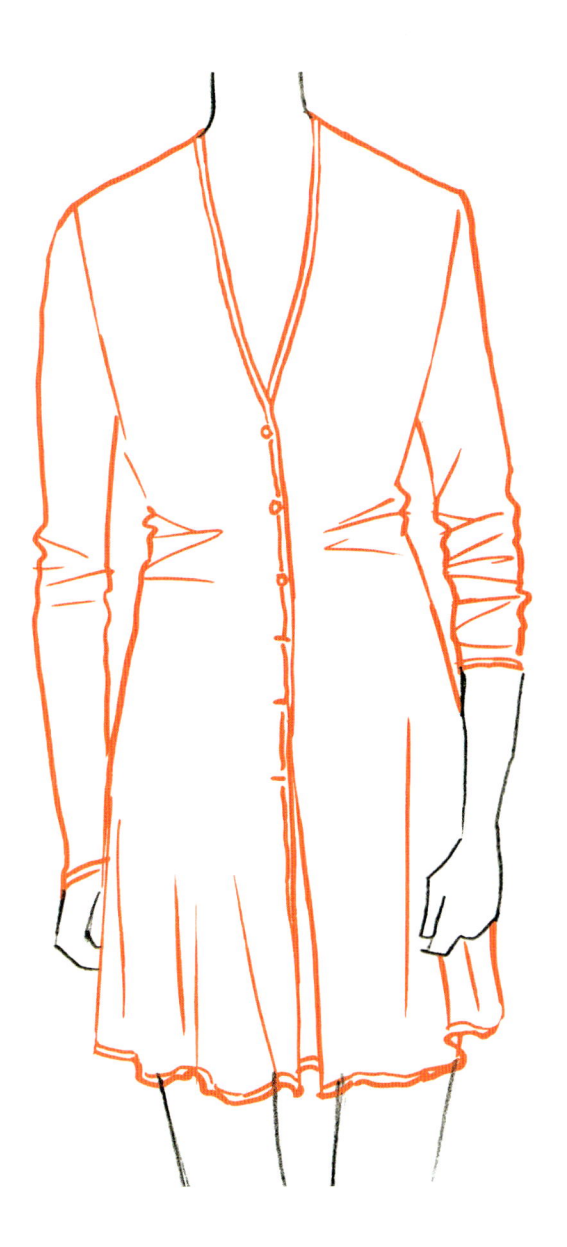

Volume

Roll-neck

V-neck

Cuffs

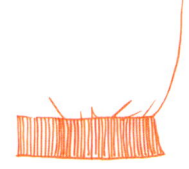

Hems

ACCESSORIES **KNITWEAR FASHION DESIGN** 133

REVAMPING THE BASICS

Every season, before planning and designing the new collections, the degree of continuity of the basic garments should be looked at. Some seasons the changes are hardly noticeable; just the neck, yarn or colour. On the other hand, some seasons there are developments in shapes and textures. However it is always essential to study the basics and the result must be fresh and original, without ever losing the core concept of the garment being revamped, as it is vital that it is still recognisable as the original piece. There are only a few basic pieces of clothing to consider: cardigans, cardigan sweaters, roll-necks, round-necks, V-necks, twinsets and polo necks. This section gives just a few examples of some ideas on how to revamp them and, at the same time, offers a general overview of current revamped basics. The ideas are supported by figurative illustrations that, together with the drawings, help to better understand the concept of the garment.

POLO SHIRT

The polo shirt is a garment that was first created for tennis and golf. Nonetheless, over the years, it has been adapted for all sectors and fashions. The defining feature of the polo shirt is the collar. For this reason the way to revamp this piece of clothing always begins with the neck, where the shape is modified every season but without losing its original character. It can be made longer or wider, or conversely it can be made to be very small or narrow, while remaining a shirt collar. The shape of the garment, the yarn and the gauge can also be changed according to taste. Amongst other items of clothing you can make polo dresses, polo jackets and polo vests. The pattern is not important but rather the important thing is the ability to find a modern design which interprets the polo neck motif for a particular season.

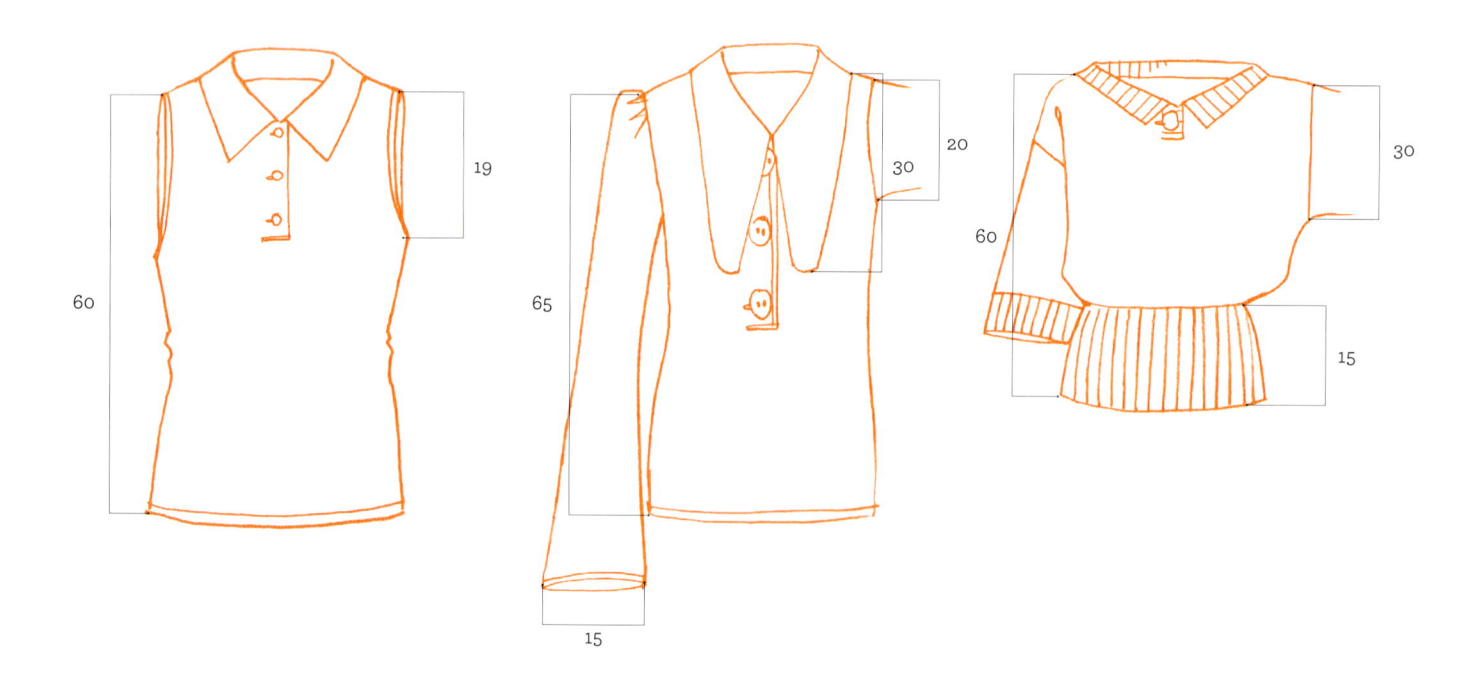

The neck is still classic, with a normal length facing. The originality is in the deep cut-away armholes, in 12 gg plain knit.

Extra-long round shirt collar. The facing, which is also long, reaches to the waist and has very large buttons. The sleeves are frilled at the top and end in tapered cuffs. The garment, knitted in 12 gg plain stitch, takes its inspiration from the style of the 1970s.

Inspired by the 1950s, the garment has kept the shirt collar, but it is cut away at the sides, with a mini facing with just one button. The wide three-quarter length sleeves give it a modern touch. The wide 4x2 ribbing contrasts with the rest of the garment, knitted in plain 5 gg stitch.

136 KNITWEAR FASHION DESIGN REVAMPING THE BASICS

REVAMPING THE BASICS **KNITWEAR FASHION DESIGN** 137

CARDIGAN I

This originated in the male sector but has long been a popular garment in women's collections, basically due to its comfort and how well it combines with other garments. It is characterised by its deep V-neck and it is usually finished with a flat band facing. It is found in all seasons and is made in all yarns and various gauges. Recently, extra large shapes such as the boyfriend- look and oversize look, have been the most popular.

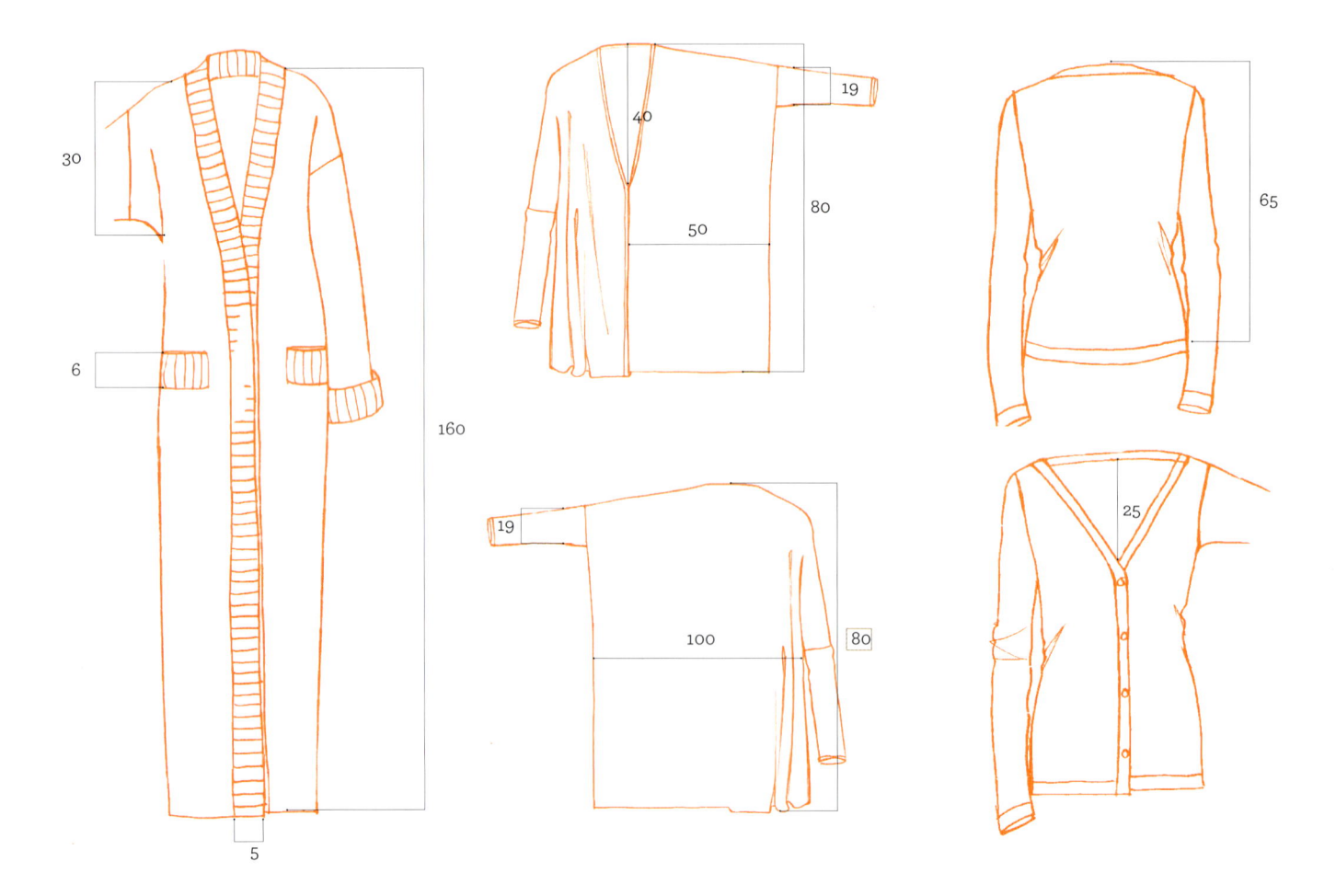

Ankle-length wrap style, without buttons, in a plain 5 gg knit.

85 cm long. Plain knit in 12 gg, very full with fitted armholes, giving it closer fitting sleeves.

Classic cardigan, with the novel detail of a back fastening.

138 **KNITWEAR FASHION DESIGN** REVAMPING THE BASICS

REVAMPING THE BASICS **KNITWEAR FASHION DESIGN** 139

CARDIGAN II

The parts of this garment - including cuffs, hems, neckline finishes and pockets - can vary, as can the colour, but, in the case of the cardigan, the interest centres on the shape and the length, two concepts which should be looked at each season.

The depth of the opening of the V-neck can be changed; it can be substantially widened or closed up, but the most important thing is that it is still a cardigan.

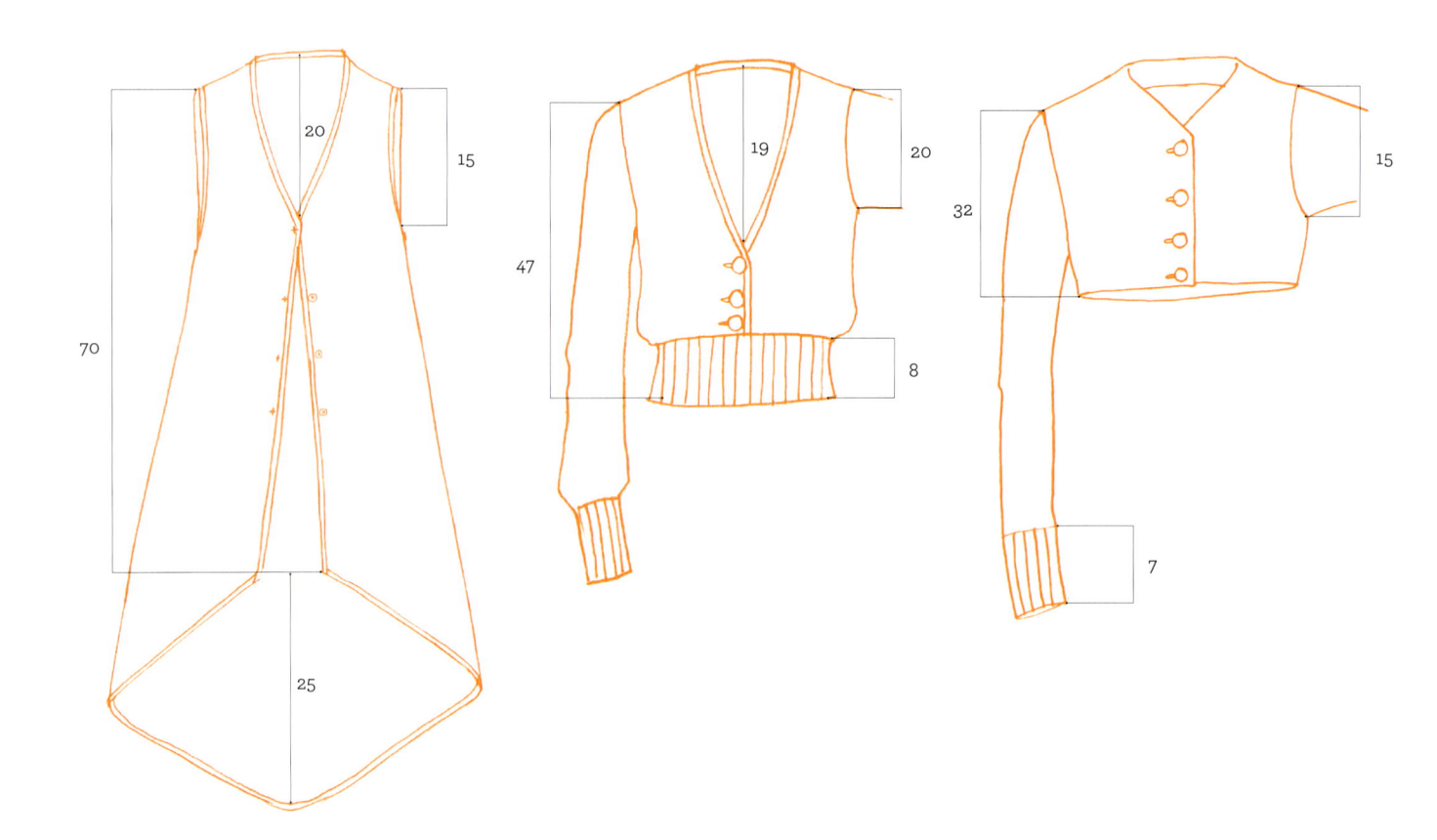

Cardigan with classic V-neck, but sleeveless and with cut-away shoulders. It shape is tapered, very roomy and asymmetrical. The finishing parts are knitted in 1 cm rib and the rest of the garment in plain stitch in 12 gg.

The innovative detail of this cardigan is found in the opening, which does not open all the way. The lapel stops at the ribbed hem making the garment a cross between a cardigan and a sweater. The cuffs are long and gathered. The garment is knitted in plain stitch in 8 gg.

The innovative feature here is that the garment is very, very short, finishing just below the bust line. It has no visible facing, there is a very high V-neck and the knit is turned inwards. The garment is made in plain knit and 5 gg.

REVAMPING THE BASICS **KNITWEAR FASHION DESIGN** 141

TURTLENECK

This is very important in winter collections. It has had some incredible variations and every season it has to be revamped again. It is very popular as it is a highly adaptable garment which can be worn with outside clothes and is a wardrobe staple. The size can be increased until it is almost oversize, or it can be made tight fitting so it fits around the neck like a second skin. It is also possible to vary the gauge, yarn and colour. It can be fastened with zips, buttons, snap fasteners or Velcro in the centre, at the side or at the back. The illustrations show three very different shapes: cape, asymmetrical and diaphanous. Three very different contrasting turtlenecks: one oversize, another in a very heavy gauge and, lastly, one which is very fine and diaphanous, however, the most important thing is that they have not lost the essence of being roll-neck garments.

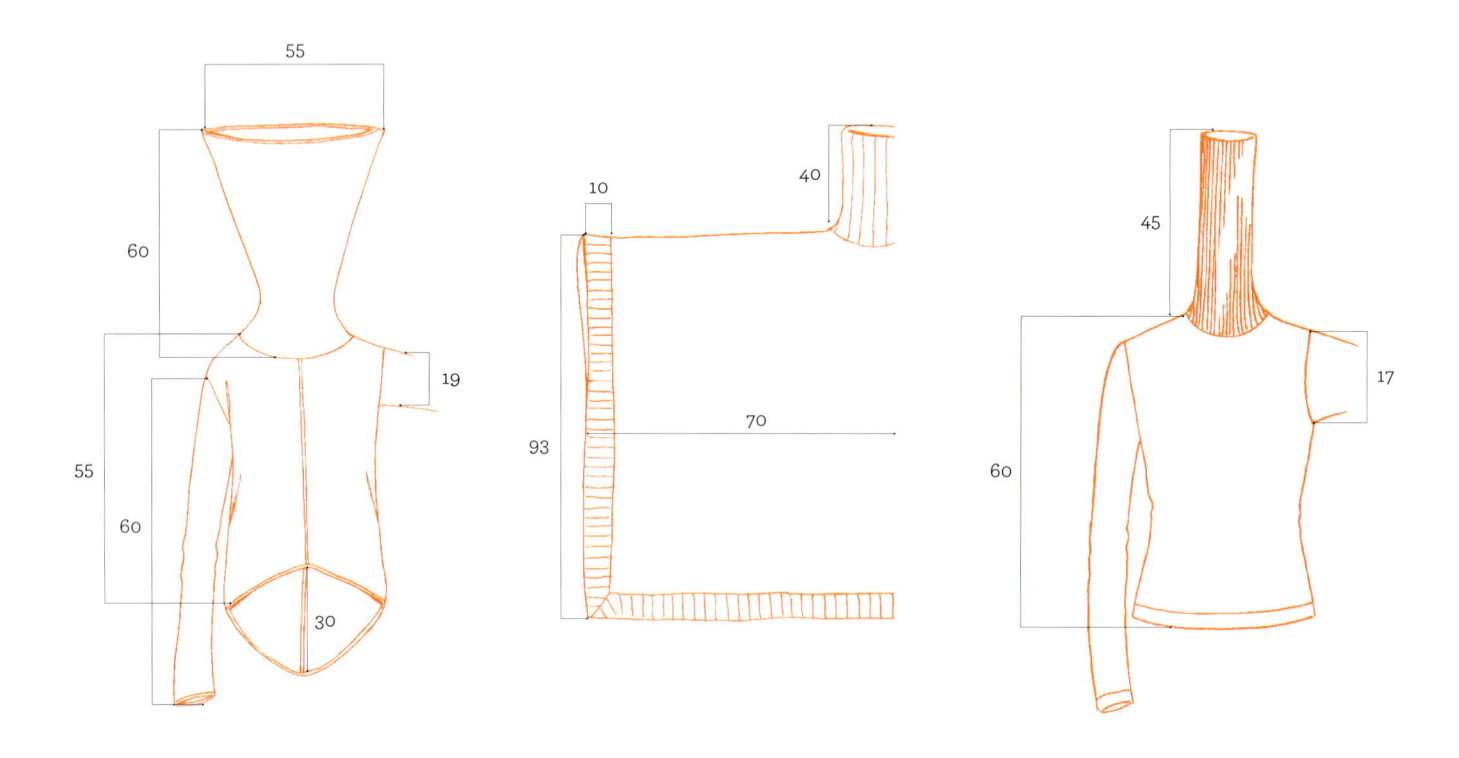

Asymmetrical garment, longer at the back and slit down the centre. Extra long sleeves. Knitted in close plain 5 gg knit. Large tapered roll-neck.

Cape-style dress, knitted in plain knit in 5 gg. Very high turtleneck and ribbing in 3 gg.

Diaphanous garment in very fine 14-16 gg. Springy bouclé yarn. Fitted high turtleneck.

REVAMPING THE BASICS **KNITWEAR FASHION DESIGN** 143

ROUND-NECK JACKET

Knitted jacket and round-neck cardigan are two of the other terms used to describe this garment. However the best known is round-neck jacket, a garment which was first seen in Alfred Hitchcock's film *Rebecca*, from which it takes its name in many languages (including Spanish), before gaining popularity all over the world. The usual design is short (55/60 cm) in fine gauge and with a narrow strip of ribbing and hems with ribbing around 7cm wide. The design is revamped every season, according to the prevailing trends; it may be lengthened or shortened until it is like a bolero jacket; its shape is made roomier or more fitted, and the neckline becomes very low or high-cut. However, the features which are most revamped in order to give it a fresh look are the gauges, stitches, colours and yarns, with the pattern staying close to the original. The illustrations show three rather exaggerated options which help to give an idea of how far the different variations can be taken.

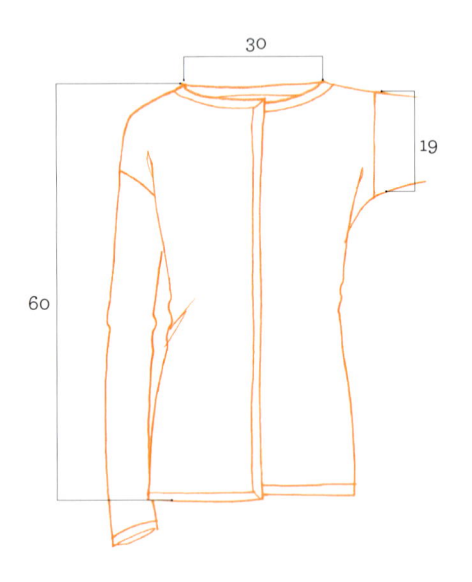

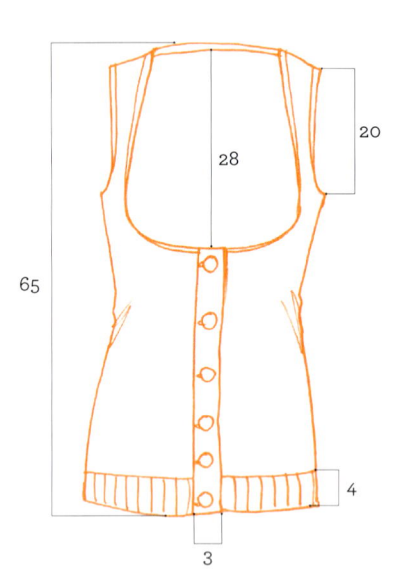

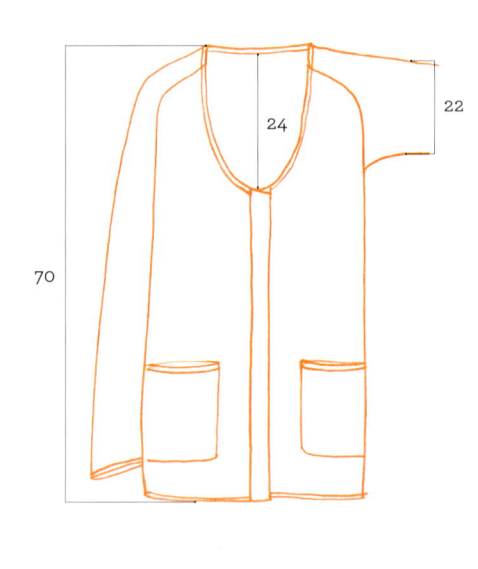

The neckline of this jacket sweater is round and quite low-cut at the sides. Buttoning under the lapel and ribbed finish.

Here the garment is very low-cut on the bust. Being sleeveless gives it a vintage bodice look. Close plain knit in 12 gg.

Deep U-neck, allowing part of the garment underneath to be seen. Ribbed finish.

144 KNITWEAR FASHION DESIGN REVAMPING THE BASICS

REVAMPING THE BASICS **KNITWEAR FASHION DESIGN** 145

ROUND NECK

The classic round neck is closed and just large enough for the head to go through, although it sometimes has a small opening at the shoulder, to make it easier to put on. Its usual finish is some kind of ribbing. Every season it is revamped to find the best variation according to contemporary trends. It can be low or very low, have a slight boat neck or be left just as it is, with the classic shape if a retro look is desired.

The finishes, such as bands around the neckline, the cuffs and hems can also vary with contrasting fancy yarns in different colours and be matt or shiny. And, lastly, the design, in this case, the neckline, will change according to the shape of the chosen garment. The illustrations show some of the changes that are currently possible.

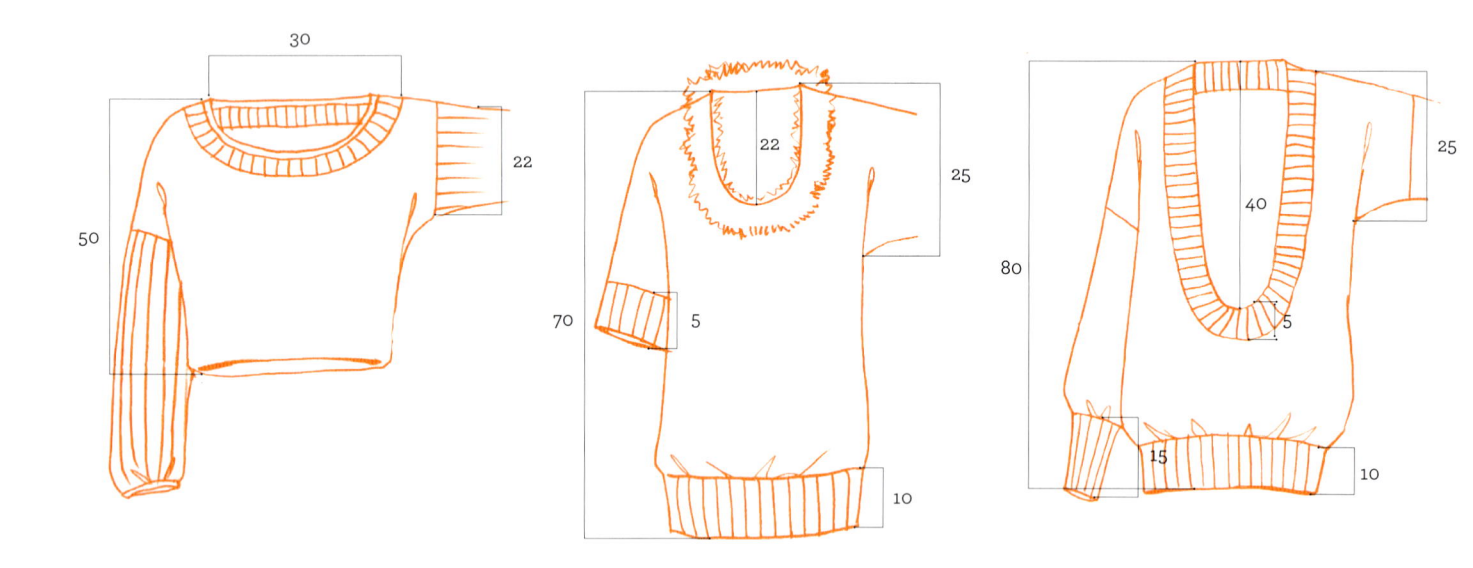

Open, boat neck, with ribbing all around. Waist length with three-quarter length sleeves.

The novel aspect of the neckline is in the choice of contrasting yarns or knits. Here a long-haired material is shown for a somewhat deep neckline close to the neck. Wide elbow-length sleeves.

Very low neck, intentionally showing the garment underneath. Roomy sweater, 90 cm long, with wide rib on the hem which gathers to give the garment a balloon shape.

REVAMPING THE BASICS **KNITWEAR FASHION DESIGN** 147

TWINSET

The twinset, from the time it came onto the market in 1940, has always been a set of two pieces in the same colour. A cardigan, around 60 cm long, worn with a short-sleeved round-neck sweater, which is usually slightly shorter than the cardigan, in a fine gauge and woollen yarn. Its usual tones are soft neutrals, blended or plain, and pastels, very typical of the twinset which came into fashion in the 1950s and 1960s.

When revamping this garment, there is no question of separating the two parts of the twinset: after all, its name is twinset for a reason - the twins belong together. Both pieces can be lengthened, made in contrasting materials or gauges, the necklines can be made lower, the sleeves of the cardigan shortened or the sleeves of the sweater underneath lengthened to three-quarter length.

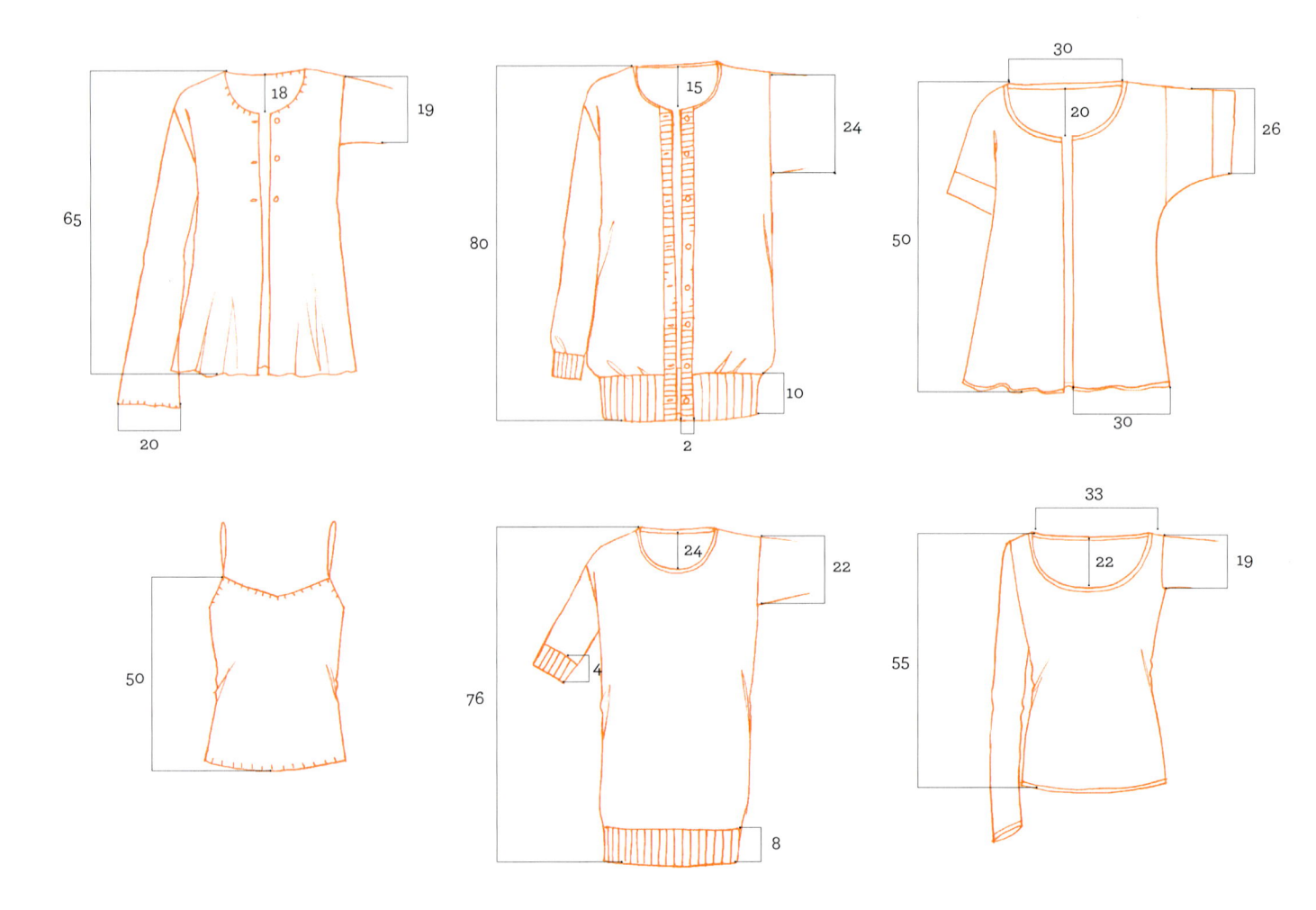

Both garments are the same colour and diaphanous, in 14-16 gg. Cardigan with tapered sleeves, and underneath a top with straps.

The most important feature of this twinset is that both pieces are practically the same length. Knitted in plain stitch in 5 gg.

This design is most notable for the short-sleeved cardigan, with ribbing in a contrasting colour, and a low round neck.

148 KNITWEAR FASHION DESIGN REVAMPING THE BASICS

REVAMPING THE BASICS **KNITWEAR FASHION DESIGN** 149

V NECK

This started off being used in menswear and, other the years, has been introduced into womenswear. It is very appealing for women as the cut of the neck can be varied giving it a greater or lesser degree of sexiness. When designing the neckline the degree of the cut can be varied: opening it or closing it right up are the most common changes. It is also possible to modify the yarns with different yarns, colours or even the width of the facings and its stitches, adjustments that can include changing the direction of the ribbing, using gauges that contrast with the rest of the garment (for example, the neck band in 3 gg and the sweater in 12 gg), even adding cables, waves, lines or other features. It involves using creativity on the neck, while ensuring that it continues to be a V-neck. The shapes of the other parts of the garment being designed must be adapted to the revamped neckline.

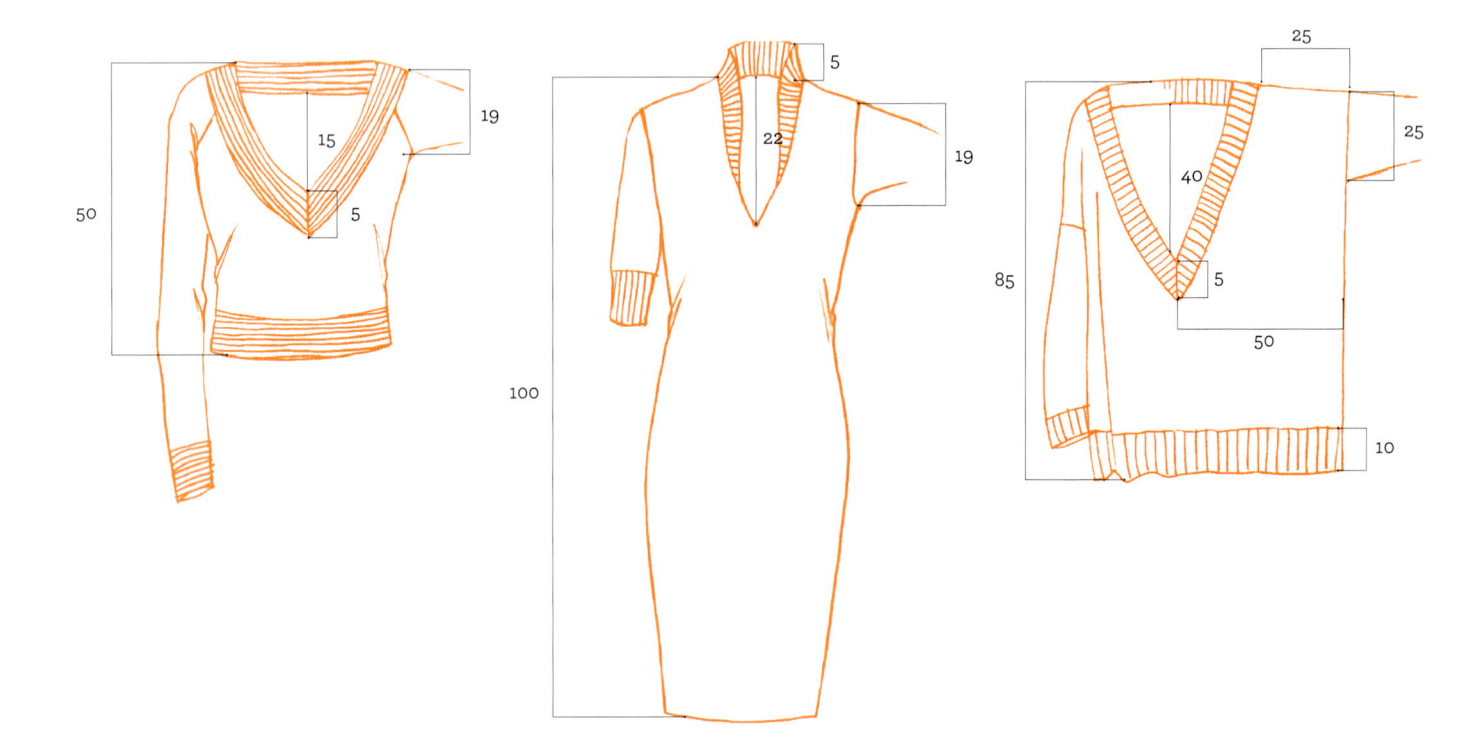

Shallow neckline that is open at the sides. Vertical ribbing on the hems, cuffs and neck. Plain knit in 5 gg.

Plain knit dress in 12 gg, with V-neck and 1940s-style neck.

Boyfriend-look or oversize garment with very low wide neck for a loose-fitting sweater in plain 5 gg knit. T-shaped sleeves.

REVAMPING THE BASICS **KNITWEAR FASHION DESIGN** 151

SPECIFI-
CATION
SHEETS

7

All garments have specifications. This is the garment's ID which contains the details of all the information needed to make it; the reference numbers, measurements (for all sizes), the colour, the yarn, the material, its accessories, and any other technical details.

SEASON:
REF:
MATERIAL:

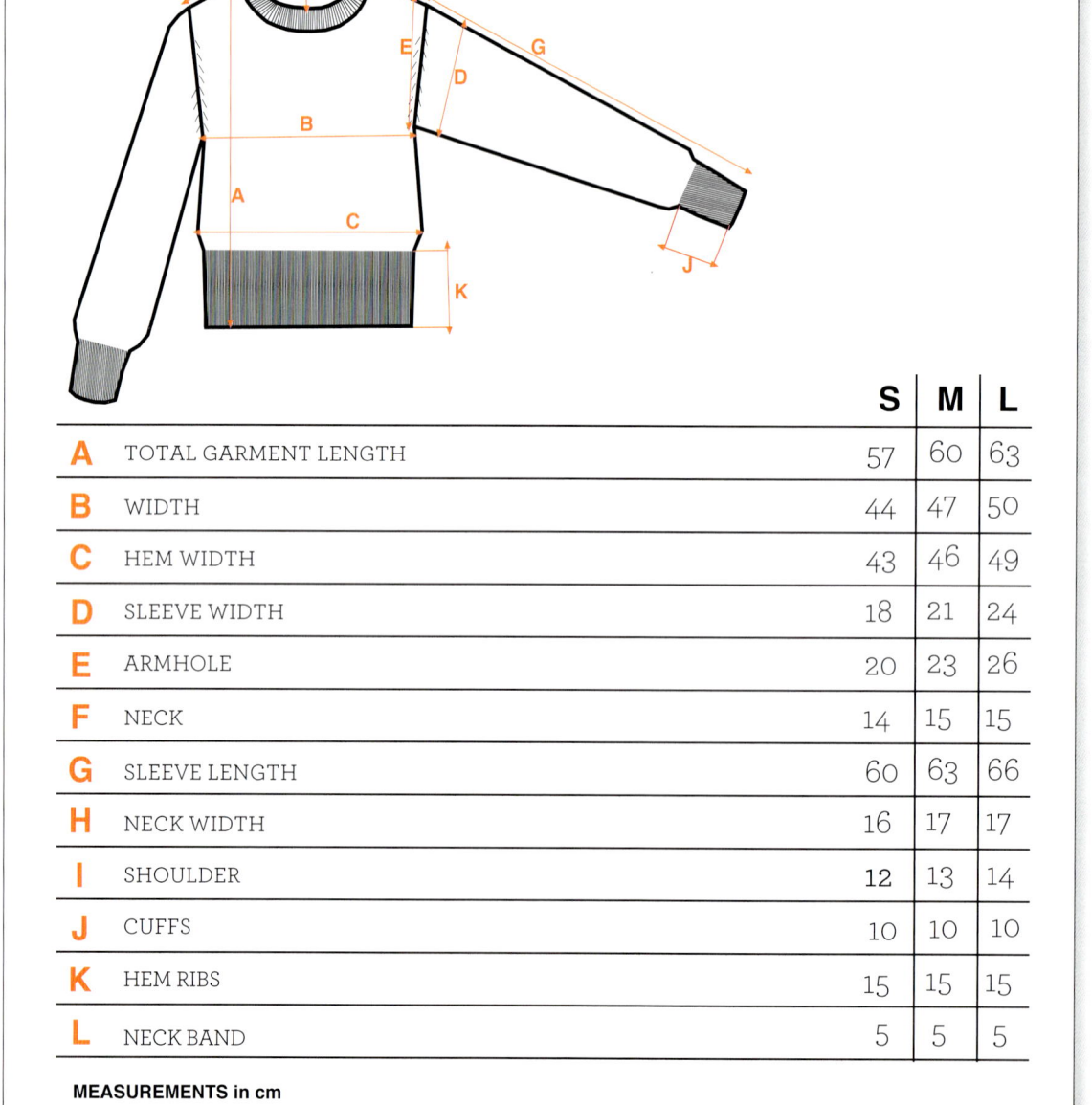

		S	M	L
A	TOTAL GARMENT LENGTH	57	60	63
B	WIDTH	44	47	50
C	HEM WIDTH	43	46	49
D	SLEEVE WIDTH	18	21	24
E	ARMHOLE	20	23	26
F	NECK	14	15	15
G	SLEEVE LENGTH	60	63	66
H	NECK WIDTH	16	17	17
I	SHOULDER	12	13	14
J	CUFFS	10	10	10
K	HEM RIBS	15	15	15
L	NECK BAND	5	5	5

MEASUREMENTS in cm

REF	MATERIAL	SEASON			
SIZES		38	40	42	44
A	GARMENT LENGTH				
B	GARMENT LENGTH				
C	ARMHOLE LENGTH				
D	SLEEVE WIDTH				
E	SLEEVE LENGTH				
F	WIDTH ABOVE RIB				
G	CUFF RIB LENGTH				
H	HEM RIB LENGTH				
I	NECK LENGTH				
J	NECK WIDTH				

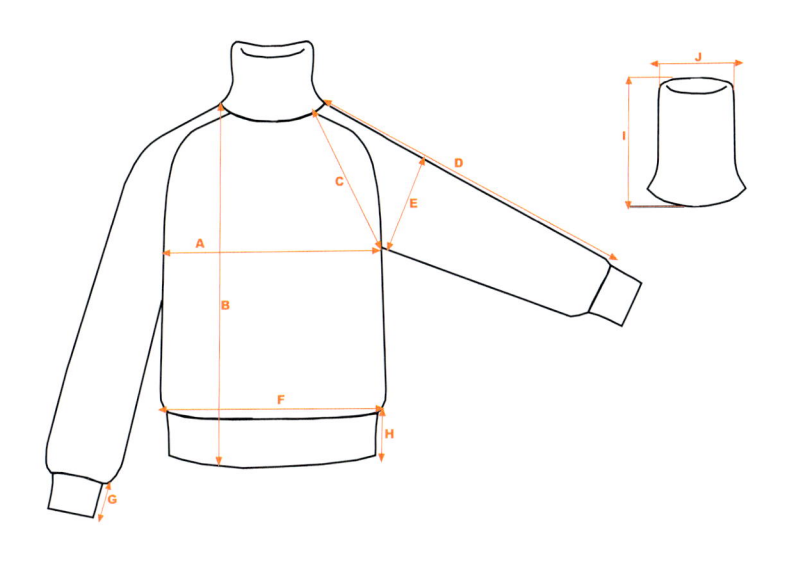

MEASUREMENTS in cm

SPECIFICATION SHEETS **KNITWEAR FASHION DESIGN**

GLOSSARY

ARMHOLE
cut in a garment corresponding to the armpit into which a sleeve is sewn to fit the body.

BLEND (REFERRING TO COLOUR)
yarn made from fibres of different colours.

CABLE STITCH
several textures of crossing layers which form various kinds of braids.

CHAIN STITCH
looped stitch on the top of a garment.

CHEQUERBOARD (ALSO CALLED CHESSBOARD)
a square design, usually composed of two colours.

COVERSTITCH
machine for overcasting the seam, making the hem and stitching.

DRAPE
the folds of a garment, used as an adornment and to give it volume.

FACING
an opening that finishes with a fastening.

FLAT STRIP
an accessory of the garment that is used as facing. It makes use of all of the needles at the front and back.

FLOAT
slip stitch with one needle bed.

FLOATING YARN
threads that are outside the fabric, like a float stitch.

FULLY FASHIONED
each of the stitches that are embedded in weaving a mesh.

GAUGE (GG)
number of a needle. The separation between the needles gives the thickness of the gauge.

HALF-CARDIGAN STITCH
combining a course with one needle bed making a stitch and the other carrying a 1x1 course.

INTARSIA
technique used to create designs in various colours.

JACQUARD
design created with punched cards. May or may not have floating threads behind.

LINKS
one needle bed knitting front and back stitches.

LOOSE KNIT
removing the needles to create a design.

MESH
the "cells" from which the fabric is formed.

NAP
chafed yarn or fabric giving a raised pile and a furry look.

NEEDLE BED
the place where the needles of the machine are located.

OPENWORK (SMALL HOLES)
changes in the fabric to create a mesh effect.

OVERLOCK
sewing machine that also cuts the edges of the cloths.

RAGLAN
cut sewn in a garment between armpit and neck to extend the sleeve from the body.

RIBBED (REGULAR)
a combination of the slip stitch of both needle beds.

ROMA STITCH
stitch where two needle beds work in half Milan stitch to create a very compact fabric.

SLUB
yarn with one end that is thick or very thick.

SINGLE END
a single yarn.

SPRINGY
ability of a yarn or fabric to return to its original position after being distorted or pulled.

TWISTING
process of winding two or more ends of the thread around each other.

WEAVE
knitted mesh.

YARN
a long continuous length of interlocked fibres, usually made by twisting.

GLOSSARY **KNITWEAR FASHION DESIGN** 157